FISHING WITH THE EXPERTS

A new look at the
Wonderful World of Angling

STILL waters and peace, perfect peace! All the joy of angling is embodied in this picture of trout fishermen at Waggoners Wells, a National Trust water at Haslemere, near Hindhead, Surrey.

FISHING WITH THE EXPERTS

A new look at the Wonderful World of Angling

EDITED BY

CHARLES WADE

CONTRIBUTORS

Conrad Voss Bark   Geoffrey Bucknall   Allen Edwards   John Goddard Frank Godsman Jim Hardy John Holden Bill Howes Arthur Oglesby   Dick Orton   Don Overfield   Leonard Parkin Michael Prichard   John Probert   Gerry Savage   Peter Tombleson Alf Walker Richard Walker

SOUVENIR PRESS LTD · LONDON

First published 1976 by Souvenir Press Ltd,
43 Great Russell Street, London WC1B 3PA
and simultaneously in Canada by
The Carswell Co. Ltd, Ontario, Canada

Reprinted 1977

ISBN 0 285 62189 0

Filmset in 'Monophoto' Baskerville 10 on 11 pt by
Richard Clay (The Chaucer Press), Ltd, Bungay, Suffolk
and printed in Great Britain by
Fletcher & Son Ltd, Norwich

CONTENTS

A wonderland of fish!

WHEREVER you live on this island, a wonderland of rich fishing is on the doorstep. A look at our map will show you the areas of sea that are a treasure house of sporting fish – delicious to eat. Also on the map are the inland waters containing coarse fish. And clearly marked for your guidance are the rivers that adequately support masses of trout and salmon.

In the southern half of the country where the sea water is warmer, shark, mullet, bass and bream thrive. But farther north it is the cod that wears the crown. Recently a new cod fishing ground, The Gantocks, was discovered over some wrecks in the Firth of Clyde. Ling grow big off the Hebrides. And congers bigger than a man are all round the coasts.

For coarse fish, take to the Norfolk Broads and the Nene and Welland area. Cornwall and Devon, particularly the gurgling streams of Dartmoor, are supreme for gay fighting trout.

Find out for yourself how good the fishing is at home. But if you have to travel in search of holiday angling, just forget about the faraway places in other lands and unpack your rod and gaff in any spot between Land's End and John o' Groats.

As far as fishing goes, you are on to a pearl without price.

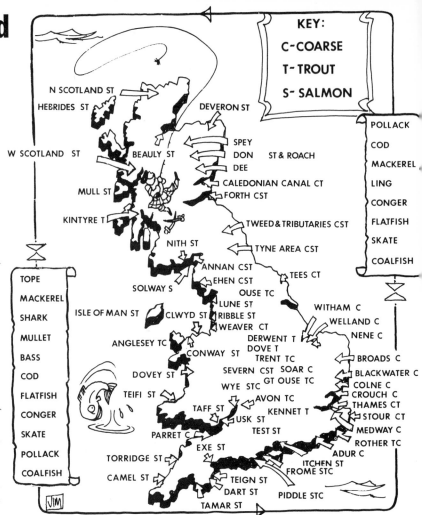

KEY:
C – COARSE
T – TROUT
S – SALMON

TOP TIP... Weighing it up

SOME of the bigger fish are too heavy to register on the normal spring balance. So find long branch, the smoother the better, support one end and hang your fish at the centre poi Use the spring balance at the free end of the stick and multiply the reading by two.

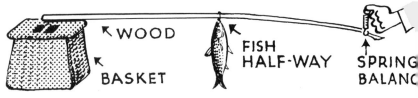

We've come a long way since fysshynge with an angle

by THE EDITOR

CATCHING fish with rod and line began in the mists of antiquity. Certainly the ancient Egyptians knew of the method; a wall painting showing a man catching a fish with a rod dates back to about 2000 BC. Early anglers fished for food and they probably found it easier to catch fish with the line suspended from a stick than by hauling the line in by hand.

Fishing for pleasure probably began in this country some time in the 15th Century, for it was in the latter part of that century that the first book mentioning the sport was published. In *The Boke of St. Albans* was an essay entitled 'A treatyse of fysshynge wyth an angle' – the work, it is thought of a Prioress, Dame Juliana Berners. Rods described were 15ft long, the butt section of willow, hazel or ash, 'as big around as one's arm', with a timber top section joined to it with hoops of iron or tin!

Today we fish with hollow glass-fibre rods that are light, responsive yet strong, with reels that are delicate gems of engineering, and that permit us to cast a long way yet have braking systems to play big fish on gossamer lines of nylon or terylene. We also go for fish that are cultivated by fish-farmers because there are so many anglers seeking sport on too few fisheries; not just because our waters cannot produce enough fish to go round, but because our way of life poisons the land and water.

Still, we are lucky that pollution is being tackled so well in this country. We still have plenty of good fishing, and the fascination and mystery of taking fish from their natural element, using our modern tackle and all the guile at our disposal, has an ever-lasting magic. Part of that magic, it has been said many times, is that one never can be certain what fish, or size of fish, will next take the bait or lure.

The more we understand about the lives of fish, about their environmental requirements at a time when modern man is changing the nature of nature, the more fascinating our sport can become. Some people can enjoy fishing for tiddlers in a murky canal with factory chimneys billowing smoke nearby and the noise of motorways and factories in their ears. Others value fishing in lovely surroundings for the peace of mind it gives them.

Match fishermen compete for cash prizes, having little time to contemplate their surroundings. Some like hunting alone or in small groups for big fish, like carp, tench, barbel and pike. Others prefer casting a fly for trout, on a reservoir perhaps, or on a raging highland river. Still others like the sea, to cast for bass from a surf-washed beach or use a boat to haul conger from rocks and wrecks.

Of all the kinds of angler, the all-rounder is the most fortunate. He can be happy whether fishing for roach in a canal, barbel in a famous river, pike in a fenland drain, trout in reservoir or river or for the many kinds of sea fish. For him there are no closed months of the year. He changes his sport with the seasons and he fishes the year round.

When we are not fishing we can think about it. We discuss, sometimes heatedly but in good humour, the pros and cons of this or that fish or technique. We tinker with tackle at home, making rods, floats, lures and flies and lead weights and nets. We can read many hundreds of books on the subject, each one different in outlook, the author of each convinced he has said the last word on a meaty subject.

Fishing is comradeship. In the schools, where many a teacher is an angler and runs special classes for his pupils. In the factories and offices, where anglers find common ground for breaks in working hours. At adult education centres, where people go to learn the art.

There are more anglers in Britain than there are footballers, cricketers, tennis and golf players. It is the largest participation sport in the country.

With such a long tradition, and so much still to be learned about fish and fishing, nobody who is an angler now, or is contemplating joining the ranks in future, could wish to be involved in a more satisfying sport.

7

THE ANGLER'S

ARTHUR OGLESBY

Arthur Oglesby has been fishing since the age of eight. He has caught more than a thousand salmon and has been described as 'one of the finest fly-fishermen in Europe'. He appears regularly on TV to discuss fishing and is also European editor of *Field and Stream*. He is a founder member of the Association of

THE RIVER SPEY ran at a low ebb, crystal clear and with the small streams bubbling over the hard, rock-girt head of the famed Pollowick pool on the Castle Grant water. A bright salmon lazily rolled in the rough water. It showed with that deliberate, porpoise-like, head-and-tail rise presenting a reasonable bet that if a fly passed over it, the fish would be a likely taker.

I carefully selected a No 8 Blue Charm, tied it on to the leader and waded out at the head of the run so that only a short cast would be required to cover the fish. The rod was a favoured 13½-footer with a No 9 floating line terminating with 30ft of level monofilament leader of 10lb test.

The fly was cast across the main current at a slightly downstream angle and the leader had been de-greased with clay so that the fly would sink an inch or two below the surface. With a few upstream 'mends' of the line, I slowed down the pace of the fly as it dragged through the water until it dangled below me and ready for another cast.

Taking a pace downstream, I cast again. The fly came round nicely and as it moved into the exact spot where I had last seen the fish, the line tightened and the rod hammered in a bow. The salmon was on!

In the early stages of play, a well-hooked fresh salmon has a few ideas of its own. As I quietly waded to the bank, the fish backed away with vicious movements of its tail. The rod bucked and

heaved, but I was safely on the bank before the fish made a searing run across to the other side of the pool with the reel ratchet making the appropriate noises. I moved downstream a little to get myself into a position where my tackle could apply side strain to the fish as it fought against both my tackle and the strong current.

This was undoubtedly the best place in which to tire the fish more quickly, but it suddenly took off again, ploughing through the white water to the head of the pool. It jumped twice and thrashed violently against the shallow rocks, but quite a few moments elapsed before the strength of the current and the pull of the rod caused it to come wallowing back into quieter water at the tail of the pool.

Without the strong current the fish now only had my tackle to fight and a good, give-and-take contest ensued before, ten minutes later, the fish lay on its side and I could lift it out by the tail. When hung on the scales it made the 11lb mark, and the hallmark of a fresh fish – sea lice – were still on it.

You could catch salmon with a wide variety of baits, flies and lures; but perhaps the greatest problem facing anglers today is that of finding access to suitable water at anything like a modest cost. Classic rivers like the Spey, Dee, Tay and Tweed all command high rentals, and even if these are not beyond your pocket there is still the problem of finding access when demand exceeds supply.

SALMON

Professional Game Angling Instructors and is chief instructor at the Scottish Council of Physical Recreation's angling courses at Grantown on Spey. Arthur lives in Yorkshire and his interests also include photography, game shooting, deer-stalking and ham radio.

Many beats are booked well in advance by long-standing tenants, and even then there is no guarantee that instant sport will be on hand. The river could be in roaring flood following heavy rain or a quick thaw on the snow-covered Cairngorms; or it could run at a mere trickle following weeks of virtual drought.

The experienced salmon angler is quite philosophical about natural causes. He has learned to take the good seasons with the bad and the moderate weeks with the hopeless. He pays his good money for nothing more than privileged access to the water and then takes pot luck on the conditions prevailing.

In choosing his selected period on the water, doubtless he would have been given a sight of the catch records for the past ten years and these records are a good barometer to indicate the best time of the year when the highest prices are paid. To be told that the Spey is a good salmon river is not sufficient. During the early months, following a hard winter, it may be that the fish will congregate in the lower beats and when a tenant on the upper Spey could fish all week for nothing. Conversely, a good beat on the lower Spey could find that most of the fish are swimming through it if the spring be mild and open.

The first problem facing any novice salmon angler, therefore, is that of finding suitable access to water which will give him a chance. Not all salmon

Author Arthur submerged and smiling in the Spey at Castle Grant.

The Oglesbys have a way with salmon. Arthur is here with one from the Lune, and Grace demonstrates a 17-pounder – the first February-caught fish from the Lune in ten years.

TEACH-IN on SALMON

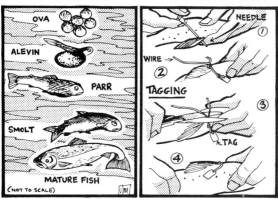

A SALMON will lay approximately 1,000 eggs (ova) for each pound of its weight, and one male salmon (cock fish) can fertilise the eggs of several females (hen fish). Born in the rivers, it spends two years in fresh water developing through the alevin, parr and smolt stages before descending to the sea. After one year in the sea it is called a grilse.

At the age of five, the salmon is mature and returns to the river of its birth to spawn.

Special plastic tags are fastened to young salmon. A hypodermic needle is inserted in the fin (1) and silver wire is twisted to a tag (2). Excess wire is cut off close (3), and to avoid discomfort to the fish, the tag and wire are pressed close to the flank (4).

water is held by private owners or wealthy syndicates, however, and there are many hotels and associations where day or weekly facilities are offered at very modest cost.

These waters do tend to get over-fished; but if the angler will persist with a few visits he will eventually learn the water and ultimately get his share of the fish being caught. Whatever other qualities you need to be a good salmon fisherman, there is no substitute for a sound knowledge of the water you intend to fish. This knowledge is not gained in five minutes or even five weeks, and in the early stages a good ghillie or local friend can be a great asset.

Having found some suitable water that fits in with your plans and your pocket, perhaps the best way to begin salmon fishing, where it is permitted, is to start with a spinner. Throughout the length and breadth of the country I suppose there are more salmon caught on a spinner than any other lure. To be really successful with a spinner, however, it is not quite so easy as it appears from a casual glance at other spin fishermen.

Ideally, you should equip yourself with the appropriate 8½ft to 9ft spinning rod and a fixed-spool reel loaded with nylon monofilament of 10lb to 12lb test. A few assorted devon minnows and Toby spoons in various sizes, together with a few swivels, complete your immediate list; but waders might be required and you may initially feel more reassured with a gaff or large landing net.

For ideal spin conditions, the river might be fining down following a good flood. The rise in water will have induced salmon to move from the estuaries or from pools in the lower beats. The river might still be a foot or two above normal height and the fish may still be running and tarrying briefly in the main lies.

In such conditions you could do worse than select a 2in black and gold devon minnow, with the additional swivel about 18in from the bait. This should then be cast across the current at the head of the main run and allowed to spin round, without winding the reel handle, until it hangs below you and out of the main current. The bait may then be quickly wound in and a pace or two downstream taken before a new cast is made.

The reason for not winding the reel handle is that you want the bait to get well down and to move over the salmon lies as slowly as possible. If the bait is retrieved after the cast is made, it does not permit

TEACH-IN on Eggs, Heads and Tails

TROUT and salmon eggs are pink and round. Laid out on plastic fluted trays (A) under clear running water, they will hatch out in 50 days if the temperature is kept at 50 °F. Barren eggs turn white and hard and have to be discarded. Fertile eggs take on a definite shape and a black spot, which is the eye, moves around inside the egg. After four weeks the egg pulsates and bulges (B). After five weeks (C) the young fish feeds on the yolk sac and it can fend for itself.

Baby salmon and brown trout look very much alike. D shows the eye which is forward of the maxillary bone scissor.

When tailing a fish from the water by hand, don't lose it again by using the wrong grip. F is right, G is wrong.

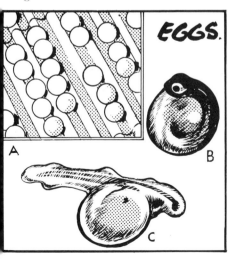

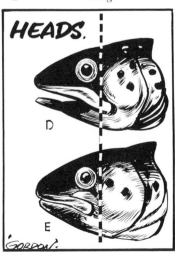

it to get down in the water and it is made to move too fast to interest anything other than a suicidal fish.

Normally, the strength of the current is sufficient to make the bait revolve, but with a very heavy bait there may be odd occasions when it will foul the bottom. The answer here is not to wind the reel handle to keep it off the bottom, but to put on a lighter bait – but not necessarily one that is smaller.

The use of additional lead can be an advantage in strong water. This may be added as a spiral above the swivel, but I find it better to wind lead wire around the trace of the devon minnow until I have on the right amount for the current involved.

There are times, later in the season, when the water has warmed above the 50 °F mark when some winding of the reel handle may be done to advantage. Under these conditions, however, the angler is more likely to fare better with fly-fishing techniques and the thrill of catching a salmon on a floating line and a small fly is greater, for me, than with any other style.

A double-handed fly rod in excess of 12ft long is normal for most rivers, and with a matching line and reel it is a simple matter to master the craft of casting. The small fly is then cast out, in much the same manner as fishing with a spinner, and is allowed to swing round in the current until it dangles below you and ready for another cast.

Providing you do not strike viciously the moment you feel a salmon take, the fish will generally hook itself. There are occasions when the salmon will nip a fly or bait and not take properly; but there is no hard-and-fast rule what to do in these circumstances. Most times I try the fish again with the same cast as previously, but you can try some experiments with smaller or larger baits or flies. Just occasionally it pays to 'rest' that fish and try for it again ten minutes later, but there is a deal of fun in finding out for yourself.

The hooking of your first salmon may well bring a highlight to your angling life. Due to your inexperience, however, it pays to be careful and not over-anxious to get it on the bank before it is fully played out. Most well-hooked fish that are lost get free for no other reason than the angler's ineptitude. During the early stages of play it pays to let the fish stay well out in the current and to keep a steady strain on it until it can be slowly worked towards the bank.

The most dangerous period comes when the fish is wallowing about on a short line. It may well then get its first glimpse of the angler and make vigorous attempts to get free. Only when the fish is lying on its side should the angler think of gaffing or netting it. If, however, there is a shelving beach on hand, it is a simple matter to lead it up the beach and pick it up by the tail.

Whatever difficulties there may be involved in getting suitable access to good water, there is nothing quite like the thrill of playing a lively, fresh-run salmon. The actual fishing can have its tedious side when conditions are bad or the fish are not co-operating; but you may never know the moment when, at the umpteenth cast, you feel that electric tug on the line and a salmon is on.

THREE-WAY GUIDE TO SALMON

AFTER one or two – but never more than three – years at sea continually feeding and putting on fat, salmon return to the river of birth to complete the life cycle. And that is when the estuary nets reap a rich harvest. Picture A shows funnel- *shaped 'putt' traps as used in the Bristol Channel. B depicts a Solway netsman with a 'heave' net straining at his shoulders. C is sometimes used on the Humber and it is called a 'lave' net.*

ESTUARY NETS

As thousands more every year take up sea angling, CHARLES WADE presents his up-to-the-minute guide to the...

COASTAL HOTSPOTS

ANGLERS are flocking to the sea in ever-increasing numbers. This branch of the sport is attracting enthusiasts at a faster rate than the rivers and lakes. Our map on page 6 lists many popular spots. The places start at Orkney and Shetland in the north, move to Thurso on the mainland and then down the east coast and right round to Ullapool.

ORKNEY AND SHETLAND: The sea around these islands is famed for big fish. May to September is best. Species caught include cod, ling, haddock, coalfish, pollack, rays, flatfish, dogfish, with a few congers in Orkney, and the chance of a halibut, though they are hard to locate. Shetland also produces whiting, turbot, tope and hake. Shore fishing on the islands has not been explored, but it could be excellent.

THURSO: This area in Caithness gives the boat angler access to some fine fishing for pollack, cod, ling, haddock, conger, common skate and the chance of a halibut. Not far away is Scrabster, also an angling centre, where shore fishing is good for conger and mullet. The coastline also yields good flatfish. Best time is May to October.

Expert afloat

CHARLES WADE is the columnist who goes afloat to catch 'em himself. Like this big 8½lb pollack he hooked off Penzance. 'A strip of mackerel is the best bait for these fish and that's what this one took,' said Charles. 'See the big eyes it has to spot a bait in deep water.'

WHITBY: The north-east coast is a noted angling area and Whitby is among the better spots. It is mostly boat fishing, but some sport is to be had from pier and quay. Further north we have Tynemouth to Eyemouth. Cod, whiting, flatfish, haddock, gurnard and small coalfish predominate. Late summer and autumn months are best.

SCARBOROUGH: Boat fishing yields cod, mainly small, good plaice and haddock. Shore fishing from the rocks and from the pier can be good. Late summer produces good plaice at times. To the south is a finger of rock called Flamborough Head, where the fishing is from the cliffs and rocks into gullies or on sand. Cod, big and small, plaice and small pollack and coalfish are taken. Boats get haddock, too.

THE WASH: Due to difficulties of access through the marshes and saltings, shore fishing is not common here. But the boat fishing in late spring and summer can be excellent, especially for tope, smooth-hounds, and rays, both thornback and sting, although overfishing by commercial interests has reduced the thornbacks to a dangerously low level. Flounders and dabs are also caught.

FELIXSTOWE: A famous centre for cod fishing from small dinghies from September – October to November is best – and sometimes through to March. Good whiting, too. Beach fishing for cod and whiting at this time is also excellent. Summer fishing is not so good, though a few good bass are taken from beach and boat. Summer also produces thornback rays, now becoming scarce due to commercial overfishing, and flatfish, with a few tope, mainly small from boats.

DUNGENESS: This famous Kent shingle promontory is famous for its shore cod and whiting from September to January, with the best months October and November. There is very deep water close to the beach. Denge Marsh, a mile to the west, is slightly shallower but also fishes in similar style. Summer months yield bass, conger, flatfish and the odd tope and turbot. Denge Marsh fishes better in summer than Dungeness, with more bass present. Boats fish offshore rocks and wrecks for big conger,

THREE TOP TIPS FOR THE SEA ANGLER

TIP ONE: On the left is a paternoster tackle for shallow beach fishing. The bubble float keeps the bait just up from the range of thieving crabs. Snoods should be of heavy grade nylon (not wire or plastic) to avoid tangles.

TIP TWO: Small sand crabs stop feeding when darkness falls – but in the daytime they steal hook baits intended for fish. An 'underwater float' that sways in the current (see below) keeps the bait out of reach of the marauding crabs.

TIP THREE: A sharp knife, a saw, some plywood and an old leather slipper make a perfect butt-pad for sea fishing. Another easy-to-make and highly effective tip, as illustrated in the diagram below.

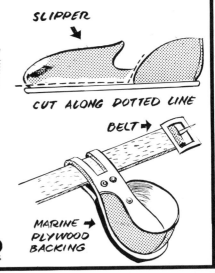

BUBBLE FLOAT

BLOOD LOOP SNOODS

TO ROD

SWIVEL

PYRAMID WEIGHT

3½" UNDERWATER FLOAT (SOFT WOOD)

MAIN LINE CURRENT

BAIT   16"

20"   WEIGHT

HARD LUCK!

SLIPPER

CUT ALONG DOTTED LINE

BELT

MARINE PLYWOOD BACKING

TEACH-IN on Safety

WATCH it, you sea anglers! Make sure you look for the spines and points of certain fish when handling a catch.

The Dragonet has no scales. This fish is found all round the coast and often buries itself in the sand. Beware of the vicious top spine.

Gurnards are good to eat. When taking them off the hook, fold down the dangerous back fin. Bass have spines on the fins and a spiked edge to the gills. Weevers carry venom in the pointed back fins.

The Spur Dogfish is capable of lashing with its sail-like tail in such a way that it folds the angler to the bony spikes which are shown on the forward edge of each back fin.

dogfish, turbot, tope and pollack in summer. Some big cod remain on offshore marks in summer, too.

HASTINGS: Can provide very good offshore boat fishing, similar species and seasons to Dungeness. There are more tope and turbot here on sandy ground and on the rough patches to the east and west. Some exceptional pollack is taken from wrecks well offshore at times. Shore fishing (October to December) produces cod and whiting. In summer the shoreline east and west, particularly east to Rye, yields good bass, soles and some conger. Hastings Pier can fish well in summer and autumn months. Mullet fishing can be good on the pier in summer.

NEWHAVEN: Provides excellent boat fishing. From October to January is best for big cod, whiting and spur-dogfish. Breakwater and East Pier also produce cod and whiting at this time, plus flounders. Summer boat fishing is good for conger, pollack, rays, big dogfish, tope, turbot, black bream and flatfish. Some big cod also hang on in summer offshore on wreck marks. Summer shore fishing can be good for bass, conger and mullet, plus flatfish, from breakwater and East Pier. On the beaches at Seaford and Cuckmere Estuary, good bass and conger are taken. Some sea trout, which run into the River Ouse, are taken spinning with bar-spoons from East Pier in June to September.

LITTLEHAMPTON: Boat fishing is similar to that of Newhaven, but black bream swarm on to Kingmere Rocks and chalky rough ground from late May to August and this is a special attraction for light-tackle anglers. The gantry on the west side of the River Arun estuary produces big bass from May to early October. Beaches to the west also produce bass and flatfish, especially at night. Mullet run into the river from late May and are catchable in the harbour at high water slack among the boats.

15

THE EDITOR AT WORK!

CHARLES WADE in action ... just to prove that editors are not all talk! Charles, seen here landing a mackerel off the Orkneys, is a third generation angler. He was Director of the Anglers' Co-operative Association, but now devotes much of his energy to two columns each week for *The Sun*. Says Charles: 'I may retire at the age of 60 ... and spend the next 40 years just fishing!' He is happily married, has two grown-up daughters – and they can all cast a decent line, he adds.

ISLE OF WIGHT and SOLENT: Excellent fishing from boats. In autumn and winter, the waters south and west of the island produce big cod, whiting and spur-dogfish and some thornback rays. In summer, shark fishing is popular and big porbeagles are taken, with the chance of the occasional thresher. At this time, too, there are good common skate, thornback rays, conger, black bream, tope, turbot, bass and flatfish. The shores yield good bass, flatfish and some tope (Lepe and Park beaches in the Solent) during the summer. Rocky areas produce conger, too.

POOLE: This vast natural harbour fishes well in late spring and summer for bass, flatfish and mullet with light tackle from small boats and the shore. Just outside the harbour, the Training Bank yields good big bass at times. Offshore boat fishing in summer yields tope, turbot, thornback rays, dogfish, pollack and flatfish, and a few modest shark.

WEYMOUTH and CHESIL BEACH: A good boatfishing area. Shambles Bank, which used to produce turbot in quantity, has been over-fished by commercial interests but it still yields turbot, tope and plaice, while offshore areas around Portland produce common skate, stingray, thornback ray and black bream. There are good conger marks, too,

particularly off Lulworth. Dogfish, pollack and coalfish are also taken in season. Shore fishing can be good over a wide area for bass and conger, and mullet are taken off the rocks and piers. Chesil Beach, a shingle mound giving way to deep water, provides beach fishermen with many species, including bass, conger, big dogfish and flatfish. Cod are also taken from the bank in winter.

TORQUAY: Shore fishing for bass, wrasse, conger and mullet can be good from rocks and piers (May to October). Offshore boat fishing on rock and wreck marks is wonderful with conger, tope, pollack, ling, turbot, cod and shark among the species. The boats can reach the Skerries Bank off Dartmouth quite quickly and turbot, flatfish and big plaice especially figure in catches made on the drift.

BRIXHAM: Boats from here fish the Skerries, too, but it is the offshore fishing on wrecks and rocks which has made Brixham famous. The results are very similar to those made from Torquay. Shark fishing is also carried out from Brixham. The shore fishing can be good, too, the harbour yielding good bass, conger and mullet. Other shore-caught fish include wrasse, pollack and flatfish. Season: May to November.

PLYMOUTH: A similar offshore fishing to that

of Torquay and Brixham. The Eddystone Reef is a popular mark where, in addition to conger, pollack, ling and cod, big bass are taken among the rock pinnacles. Shore fishing for bass, thornback rays, pollack, conger, wrasse, flatfish and mullet. Shark fishing is done. There is an excellent angling centre at The Barbican, where sound advice is offered.

FOWEY: This Cornish centre produces good shark fishing as well as excellent offshore fishing for big pollack, ling, conger, cod, red bream, turbot and several other species. The shore fishing is also good, especially for bass in the estuary and on the shores in the neighbourhood where mullet, wrasse, conger and flatfish are taken. Bass fishing goes on into October.

MEVAGISSEY: There is good shark fishing, as well as good offshore fishing for many of the fish caught from other West Country centres. Bass fishing can be good from the beaches and conger

TEACH-IN on CRABS

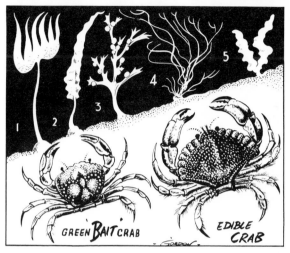

GREEN *BAIT* CRAB   EDIBLE CRAB

TEACH-IN on FLATTIES

SEA FISH tend to go bad much quicker than freshwater fish. So if your catch is for the pot, gut it as soon as it is caught (see below). Sole and other flatfish are better if cooked with the skin off. An hour or two on a cool slab will dry off the slime.

Use a sharp knife and discard the gills (A). Scrape out congealed blood. Loosen the skin with finger and thumb (B) and peel (C).

A baited-spoon tackle rig (D) is a good method of fishing for flatties by dragging over a sanded sea bed.

MOST prowling sea fish greedily devour whole crab baits. Anglers specialise in collecting the soft-shelled 'green' crab because it is found near damp sand and seaweed when the tide goes out. It can live quite happily on dry land between tides. The 'edible' crab has a wider shaped shell and, though liked by fish, it is mostly eaten by fishermen.

When worm baits are hard to come by, they can be eked out by draping the hook with part worm and a sliver of weed. Sea weeds get tougher and thicker stemmed as the sea gets deeper. Reading from left to right are Kelps, Bulb-rooted (1) and Cow Tail (2). Bladder Wrack (3) and Sea Thong (4) are red weeds. Sea Lettuce (5) is a green weed which thrives in shallow water just below the eel-grass plant line.

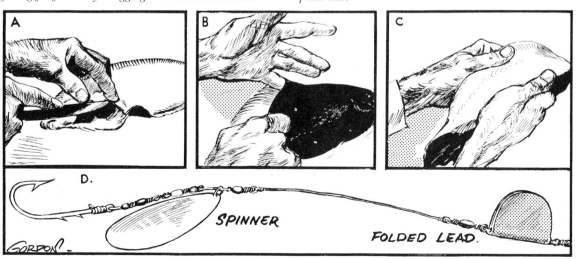

SPINNER   FOLDED LEAD.

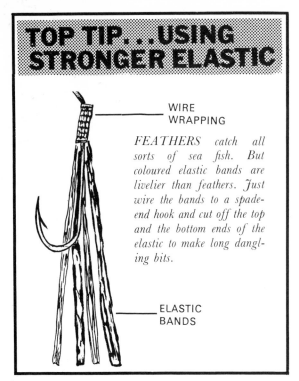

and mullet fishing from the harbour can be excellent.

FALMOUTH: Superb shark fishing is to be had out of this famous harbour, including blues, porbeagles and makos. All the West Country deep-water species are taken here, including common skate. The Manacles Rocks produces excellent sport. The shore produces bass, conger, pollack, wrasse and flatfish.

NEWQUAY: Another shark-fishing port where there is also good offshore boat fishing for many West Country species. Good shore fishing for bass and pollack. Mullet, flatfish and conger are also caught.

APPLEDORE ESTUARY: This area is famous for its bass fishing on the bar in the estuary, where the fish shoal thickly from May to the end of October. Trolling, spinning or driftlining with sand-eel from small boats is the accepted technique. Nearby the fishing in Bideford Bay is good, but due to tidal conditions, the area is best fished from Clovelly.

WESTON-SUPER-MARE: Shore fishing from May to October for bass, flounders, soles, thornback ray, dogfish, plus the usual pouting and silver eels.

TEACH-IN on WHITING and CO.

THE BEST *time to catch whiting is at night when the moon is shining. They are then in the very shallow water where the waves break. Whiting are soft of flesh and the skin is greyish yellow.*

Bass should have the scales removed before cooking. Turbot and halibut are sometimes mistaken for each other. The

halibut is deep-bodied and a big bone runs through the centre as shown in the cutlet. Only the wings of a skate are worth eating. The flesh is rosy and slightly corrugated.

Experienced sea anglers are now very conservation minded. Small fish, and also those not needed for the pot, are returned to the water.

There are sandy beaches and two rocky peninsulas, Brean Down and Sand Point, where congers are caught. Boat anglers catch similar species. Cod and whiting arrive in October and remain until the end of March. Cod run to double figures in good years. Dinghy anglers should keep within the bay owing to strong offshore tides.

SWANSEA to TENBY: This area produces vast numbers of tope from boats fishing between a mile and eight miles offshore. Also taken are thornback rays, and there are good pollack rocks well out. Sharks are also becoming more of a proposition, both blues and porbeagles, some having been taken within a mile of the shore. Shore fishing can be excellent for bass and there are several places on the shore that yield lots of tope from May to September. Winter fishing is poor.

LLEYN PENINSULA and ANGLESEY: North Wales produces excellent shore fishing in general, but the shallow storm beaches of the Lleyn Peninsula are perhaps the best for surfcasting for bass. Tope and flatfish are also taken. Anglesey and the Menai Straits produce good bass and tope, with flatfish, pollack, wrasse and codling also being taken. The varied shoreline permits a variety of methods. Boat fishing yields tope, rays, turbot, common skate, plaice, pollack, coalfish, dogfish and conger. Mullet also figure in shore catches.

BIRKENHEAD (for Liverpool Bay fishing): North of Anglesey the fishing deteriorates until the Solway Firth is reached, but some larger boats fish the offshore area to the north of Anglesey from Birkenhead. They also go out in deep water and have had good fishing for tope and have contacted some sharks. Flatfish are also taken, plus some cod.

WHITEHAVEN: Situated on the southern side of the Solway Firth, Whitehaven commands a stretch of coast between Ravenglass to the south and Maryport to the north. The fishing is not outstanding but keen anglers fare creditably with some bass, flatfish, especially flounders and thornback rays. Tope can be taken while boat fishing. Smallish cod and coalfish make up the rest of the catches.

SOLWAY FIRTH area: The North Atlantic Drift carries warm water into this area, and with it come bass. It was only a few years ago that bass fishing was seriously carried out here from the shore and some good fish, into double figures, have been taken. Tope fishing is also good in this area, mainly from boats, though a few have been caught from the shore. Flatfish, cod, and modest coalfish are also caught. Mullet fishing from the shore is good.

ISLE OF ARRAN: The area has sheltered waters where safe fishing in small boats may be enjoyed, and its marine life is extremely rich. On the open sand and mud sea-bed, haddock, cod and some good plaice are taken, while the rocky areas produce good pollack, haddock and cod inhabiting gullies between rocks. Among other species to be caught are whiting, thornback rays, some skate and small congers. Most of this is boat fishing, and off the island of Pladda there are tope in early autumn. Shore fishing needs exploring and could be good.

CLYDE AREA: In recent years, the Gantocks mark in the Clyde off Dunoon has become famous for its big cod taken on jigging heavy lures. Many fish of more than 30lb have been caught. Small boats are used extensively. Species in the Clyde include haddock, whiting, dogfish, some skate, conger, coalfish and tope. Some shore fishing is done from the rocks into deep water and from beaches and piers.

ULLAPOOL: This harbour on Loch Broom is famous for big skate, taken from boats fishing the Summer Isles grounds, Horse Island and other named marks. Big conger, ling, cod, pollack, coalfish, haddock, tope, dogfish, flatfish and whiting are taken. Many skate over 100lb are taken, and although the offshore grounds are best, there is a skate mark not far from the pier. Big conger are taken from the steep shores of Loch Broom itself, which also yields good flatfish and coalfish.

HERE'S THE METRIC WEIGH

HERE'S an easy-to-remember conversion to metric figures to calculate quickly the weight and length of the fish you catch. Each one-quarter ounce of weight is equal to seven grammes, and every two inches in length is equal to five centimetres.

Those vital blows

FORCE 4 wind is a moderate breeze of 13 knots. But you sea anglers can suffer much worse blows! For example: Force 5 – fresh breeze 18 knots; Force 6 – strong breeze 24 knots; Force 7 – moderate gale 30 knots; Force 8 – fresh gale 37 knots; Force 9 – strong gale 44 knots; Force 10 – whole gale 52 knots; Force 11 – storm 60 knots; Force 12 – hurricane 68 knots. Then you've got problems!

TEACH-IN

TRY GIVING THEM AN OILY INJECTION!

MUSSEL *flesh (A) is a tasty bait for sea fish. Fasten the bait to the hook with strands of sheep's wool or nylon thread. Dead lug and ragworm (B) can be made more tempting when injected with cod liver oil or pilchard oil.*

Sinkers can be the most costly items. Crevices, dredger chains, and the supports of piers get festooned with them. 'Farewell' sinkers (C) can be utilised by tying some pebbles or sand in a plastic bag or paper hanky.

TRANSATLANTIC SWIM IS THE EEL END

18" LINE FROM HOOK TO SWIVEL

LINK SWIVEL — LINE TO ROD — PEAR SHAPED LEAD.

FEMALE *eels three feet long are relatively common, but the male does not grow to more than 20 inches. At breeding time the eel takes on a silvery sheen, but normal colouring is a deep greenish-yellow.*

Although the greater portion of its life is spent in fresh water, the eel is born in the sea and returns there to breed. In the autumn, adult fish leave the rivers and swim across the Atlantic to the very deep Sargasso Sea. After spawning, the eels die.

The larvae, swept along by ocean currents, take $2\frac{1}{2}$ years to get back into Europe. During the trip, they change into elvers and are no thicker than a darning needle. They enter the rivers by the million, in shoals which turn the water into a black, wriggling mass.

Eels from East and West mingle on the same spawning ground, but experts tell us that the offspring always go back to their own hemisphere (see illustration at top of picture).

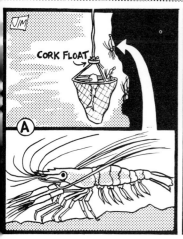

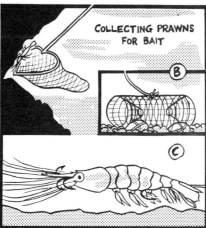

CORK FLOAT

A

COLLECTING PRAWNS FOR BAIT

B

C

Prawn baits send 'em mad!

BASS go really mad on fresh prawn baits. And salmon are sent frantic if a whiskered boiled prawn crosses their path. To collect the baits, work on a rising tide because prawns keep coming inshore at the front of the tide.

The drop net is baited with a bit of old fish, and it should be worked under every ledge (picture A), where the prawns position themselves 'upside down'.

The hand net should be heart-shaped and pushed into submerged reefs and weeds (picture B). The trap is just a wire cage with funnels.

When baiting up (picture C), camouflage the treble-hooks by fixing them amid the whiskers and the legs of the prawn.

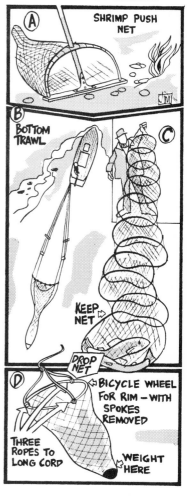

A
SHRIMP PUSH NET

B
BOTTOM TRAWL

C

KEEP NET

DROP NET

D

BICYCLE WHEEL FOR RIM – WITH SPOKES REMOVED

THREE ROPES TO LONG CORD

WEIGHT HERE

Here's a TOP TIP for four ounces

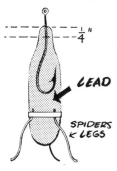

LEAD

SPIDERS LEGS

FOUR-OUNCE weights are a good standby when sea fishing. Make your own by taking an empty sparklets bulb, and sawing off the top to form a neck opening. Then saw the rest in half – lengthwise. After inserting an old eyed-hook, place the two halves of the mould into a vice. Fill with lead and when cool, tap off the mould. The wires can be added when fishing over rocks – the wire comes free and no weights are lost.

ALL ABOUT NETS...

TO GATHER shrimps for bait, use a push net (A). A wooden frame keeps the mouth of the net open. Large-scale commercial fishing is mostly done with trawl nets. Picture B shows a bottom-trawl in operation. Sometimes two trawlers will pull a single net, and this method is called mid-water trawling.

Sea anglers who fish from piers are now beginning to use long keepnets (C) which are capable of keeping the catch fresh in the water whatever the state of the tide.

Big fish, lobsters and crabs, can be lifted to the pier by means of a simply made drop-net (D).

LINCOLNSHIRE FOR PIKING PERFECTION

EVERYONE knows about Wombling, new though it is, but how many anglers know about delphing – the style of winter fishing which is certain to put the angler in contact with plenty of pike, give lots of exercise, foster good relationships with Common Market anglers and guarantee the wife a fish supper?

The name, of course, gives the game away, especially to East Anglian or Lincolnshire anglers for the delph is but another name for a drain. Lincolnshire is criss-crossed with long ribbons of water, which is pumped from the land and pushed down the delphs and into the older natural waterways for disposal into the sea. They are for the most part shallow, fertile, well stocked with coarse fish of all types and provide a perfect food chain for predators like the pike, perch and latterly the zander. Man, the supreme predator, comes along as the end of the chain and gets his entertainment by taking the pike from the waters in a sporting manner.

The tackle for delphing is simplicity itself. The ideal rod for the game is a 7–8ft medium spinning rod, a fixed spool reel loaded with 8lb breaking-strain line, a few swivels, some alasticum wire and treble hooks. The only other requirement is bait, and for this there is nothing better than a pound of sprats from the market.

The fishing, like the tackle, is simple. First stretch one of the sprats out flat on the ground. Measure out about a foot of the single strand trace wire and whip one of the size 8 trebles on to the end. Fix this first hook into the wrist of the sprat's tail. A second treble hook should now be slipped down the trace and fixed in position by taking one turn of the trace wire around the bend of one arm of the treble.

This second hook should be fixed so that one prong of the treble may be hooked through the eyes of the deadbait but – and this is most important – there should be no curve in the baitfish. Providing that care is taken at this stage the bait will behave as it should in the water. An incorrectly set up bait will not deter a feeding pike from striking but it will prevent the angler from inducing a semi-dormant pike to strike, which is what delphing is all about. Complete the rig with a swivel at the end of the

ALLEN EDWARDS claims to be a born angler, since his birthday falls on the opening day of the coarse fishing season. Born in 1930, he was educated at King Edward VI Camp Hill Grammar School where, among other things, he was taught to fish by 'Ginger' Brain. His first catch consisted of thirteen roach and he has been catching fish, of all sorts, ever since, including several roach over the magical 2lb mark and pike of over twenty pounds. He regards himself as a typical pleasure angler and maintains that life is competitive enough without introducing the element into angling.

Has lived in Nottingham for twenty years and knows the river Trent well, together with the waters of Lincolnshire. Spends time raising funds for the pollution fighting fund of the Anglers Co-operative Association, which he regards as the most important body in angling. He is an N.F.A. qualified instructor and runs courses at the National Water Sports Centre at Holme Pierrepont. Likes to talk about fishing and broadcasts regularly as BBC Radio Nottingham angling correspondent.

by ALLEN EDWARDS

trace and, having joined the trace to the reel line with a half blood knot, the fishing can begin.

Now this is where the exercise comes in! Some delphs are miles long, many are featureless and the angler's work-out comes from prospecting the water. The trick is to spend time quietly working up the delph casting and retrieving, searching out a piece of water and moving on all of the time.

The pike are not spread evenly along the drains but gather, like wartime U-boat packs, around the shoals of bait fish. The first objective is to locate a gathering of the pike, the second is to clobber as many as possible of the pack including the bigger female fish. The problem then becomes one of covering as much water as possible but in such a manner as to entice a strike from even the most replete of pike.

This is why it is so important to take great care when mounting the bait fish; if this is right, a three-times pattern of casting will prove to be the most effective method of covering long stretches of water in an efficient manner, producing a better-than-average chance of a strike from the pike. The key to the casting pattern is accuracy, for the aim is to cast just three times into each likely holding spot – once to rouse the pike, twice to set his fins a-quiver and the third time to induce him to strike.

The angler can afford to be a bit slap-happy with the retrieve on casts one and two, but care is required for the third. That one should be the final straw to any self-respecting pike and it will be if the angler visualises the action of the bait.

The little fish should be allowed to settle almost to the bottom. The reel pick-up should be engaged and the rod tip should be raised at the same time. This has the effect of causing the bait to rise in the water in a long, steady draw. If the rod tip is then dropped smartly to one side the bait will hold, enticingly, in one spot for a few seconds and will then begin to settle back to the bottom. The action is repeated until the bait is under the rod tip, as the pike will sometimes follow a bait worked in this manner for some way before striking. Usually, however, the angler will have simulated the action of an escaping prey, which appears to trigger a reflex action on the part of the pike to grab the bait while the going is good.

No matter what the size of pike, by the way, an instant strike should be made with this rig. There is absolutely no need to wait for the pike to turn the bait and to swallow it head first.

This is the reason for stipulating a medium spinning rod. A light rod will easily cast the small unweighted bait across the narrow waters and it will work the bait in an adequate fashion to induce the strike, but it will not drive the hooks home into the bony jaws of Master Jack Pike.

The delphs then provide exercise, good fishing and bags of fresh air (since there is nothing but flat land and the sea between them and the Urals), but what about the good relations with the Common Market? The fact is that were it not for a Dutchman, one Cornelius Vermuyden, there would not be any delphs to fish in. He, with the encouragement of Charles I, began the massive task of converting the Fenlands into prosperous farmlands in 1626. He carried through the first works in five years at a cost of £55,000. It did not do him much good in the long run, because although he beavered away until around 1639 he finished up in a debtors' prison.

As an English angler I tell my Dutch friends that while, in my view, their cheese is fit only for chub bait, we do owe our Fenland fishing to them. I think they regard it as a compliment; they always go very quiet afterwards!

Not that I have anything against the Continentals, except perhaps that they eat a lot of freshwater fish. That might seem strange, since I have said that delphing with the sprat is one way of guaranteeing a fish supper. The pike, however, is under pressure and I do not advocate that anglers add to the pressures in an indiscriminate manner by adding the pike to our already over-long list of victuals. The odd fish taken here and there will not endanger the species' future, but if all anglers took away the pike which they caught there is no doubt that the fish would become rare in a very short time.

Care should be taken in the playing and landing of the fish. Some anglers will net their pike, others will use the gaff. In each case it is better to wait until the fish is fairly well played out before attempting to swing it on to the bank. A strong pike which is thrashing about is difficult to free of hooks.

It's a question of presentation

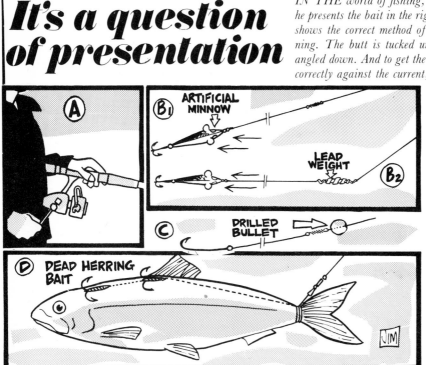

IN THE world of fishing, even a novice can be king if he presents the bait in the right way to the fish. Picture A shows the correct method of holding the rod when spinning. The butt is tucked under the arm and the rod is angled down. And to get the artificial lure (B1) to swim correctly against the current, just weight it as in B2.

A favourite method of legering for eels and other fish which take food from the bottom, is to use a drilled bullet (C). Little resistance is felt as the fish swims away with the bait.

And when after big pike, just cast out a dead herring which has been 'dressed' overall with a wire trace, and two sets of small treble-hooks, as in Picture D.

If the fish has been badly hooked, bleeding can occur and another fine fish is lost to the water.

Carrying a net can be a problem along miles of Fenland drain, especially as the main attraction of delphing is the opportunity for the angler to travel light. My own method with all but the biggest of pike is to play them out and to lift them out by grasping the fish just behind the head.

The drains and delphs of Lincolnshire and East Anglia are full of pike. The fish are highly suscept-ible to a bait worked to induce a take. Unless the wife has thrown too many bats' eyebrows into the cauldron and said a couple of extra hubble-bubbles to put a real spell on the day, I can usually depend upon getting a few fish on a day's outing.

A pound of sprats, however, is always more than enough to see the day through. With their heads pulled off, dusted with seasoned flour and popped into deep frying fat, they make a delicious plateful.

That, of course, is her guaranteed supper.

JACK FALLS FOR A SPRAT

THIS fine-looking character was taken on a legered sprat. Place: Wraysbury No. 1 Lake, Bucks. Weight: twenty pounds.

STONE THEM AND BE DAMMED!

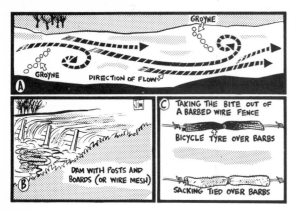

SOME stretches of water are shallow, flat and uninteresting even to fish. But improvement is simple. Groynes (A) made of heaped-up stones will alter the flow of the current and create fish-holding pools above and below the lines of stones. To prevent scouring of the river bank, build the groynes on alternate sides.

Fish just love to live near a dam where the water is deep and still above the dam, and turbulent below it. But most existing dams were built in the last century to provide power for the corngrinding mills. Many dams have crumbled away.

Anglers today can set about building their own dams (but it is wise to keep them low and adjustable in height) by using the method in Picture B.

Clambering over a barbed wire fence does damage to temper, flesh, waders and clothes. Tame the fence by closing the barbs with pliers or by wrapping as in Picture C.

THE CRUEL RIVER

ALL FISH have a cruel streak. Often they can survive only by bullying the weak. Trout get their food by lying 'in station' at a place in the river where food drifts past. The biggest fish always claims the spot at the head of the queue and takes first pick of the food.

Pike are predators which take their food by ambush. The unsuspecting victim is taken broadside and then turned to be swallowed head first (A). The special-shaped teeth (D) are adapted for the purpose.

Always, when fishing and continually casting, make sure the winch fittings (B) do not work loose. And when a fish is caught and has to be dehooked, do it as in Picture C. When the fish is safely returned to the water, it will make a good recovery.

Reading the signs in the clouds

LEARNING to read the signs of wind and cloud will take most of the hazards away from sea-fishing. Clouds are constructed of mist high up in the atmosphere. Cumulus formations resemble piles of soap suds and they signify fine weather. When the wind is offshore, be wary. Every high cliff and sea-front building creates a zone of shelter (bottom left), but nearer to the horizon a tide and wind rip (B) can prove dangerous to boat and crew.

Fog is very frightening. But if the boat is lost and without a compass, it is possible to get a bearing by using a white handkerchief and pencil. Nearing evening the sun is always in the west and the shadow will fall to the east. Before noon the shadow will fall to the west.

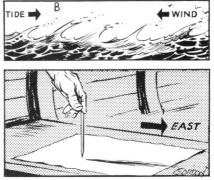

TROUT FISHING

by RICHARD WALKER

RICHARD WALKER had his first fishing article published in 1936 and is the author of seven books on angling, the first of which was published in 1951. He also holds the British carp record with a 44-pounder.

Richard was born at Hitchin, Herts in 1918 and was at Gonville and Caius College, Cambridge University. He read Mechanical Science from 1939–45, worked on night fighter radar at the Royal Aircraft Establishment, Farnborough, for many years, and is now the technical director of a firm which designs horticultural machinery. He is married with four sons.

A REVOLUTION has taken place in trout fishing in the last 20 years or so, mainly in England. In Scotland and Wales there has always been trout fishing at a cost that everyone could afford, but in England the destruction of trout streams by pollution and source abstraction so reduced the amount of trout water left that it became priced, through the effect of supply and demand, out of the reach of all but a few rich people.

The revolution was started by the construction of water supply reservoirs, which were stocked with trout and which could be fished at a cost that most anglers could afford. This led many thousands of anglers to take up trout fishing. Later, smaller man-made trout lakes were excavated all over the country, and these, though more expensive to fish than the reservoirs, are still within the reach of most to fish now and then, if not as often.

A further development has taken place in that some stretches of our remaining trout streams, instead of being let to small numbers of anglers who could fish whenever they wished, are now let on a one-day-per-week basis; this allows many more individuals to fish, though each may fish on only one allocated day of the week. All these waters depend on artificial stocking, but this is done on a few-and-often basis, so that at no time does a water hold more fish than can find plenty of food in it. The trout farmers have developed fish-food that produces fast growth and highly palatable trout-flesh.

Because so many people can now fish for trout, the tackle trade has made great strides in developing better equipment, some of it specialised to meet the needs of different kinds of trout fishing. Different rods and lines are needed for large reservoirs from what would be suitable for stream fishing. There has also been much development of new artificial flies for lake and reservoir, most of the insects on such waters being different from those found on rivers.

How should the man who wants to take up trout fishing make a start? I suggest a visit to the local tackle shop, whose proprietor does not expect to sell trout tackle to anglers who have nowhere to use it. Consequently, he will be not only willing but eager to tell the novice what trout waters are available and on what terms they may be fished. He will also be able to advise which rods, reels, lines and flies are suitable for these waters, and suggest where lessons in fly-casting may be obtained. Learning to cast with a fly-rod is rather easier than learning to swim or to ride a bicycle, and you don't have to reach a very high standard in order to be able to catch some fish, though obviously the better you become the more fish you will catch.

The anglers you find on reservoirs are a very

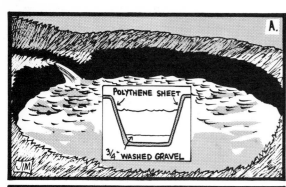

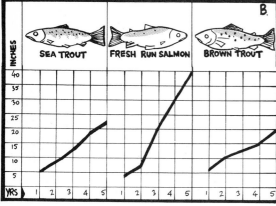

TEACH-IN: Here's how to raise your own fish

YOUNG FISH can be reared successfully in any stream, pond or ditch, where there is a constant supply of clean running water. A natural spring is the ideal 'feeder'. To construct your own rearing pool (picture A), make it about 18ins deep and install a small circulating pump. Line the pool with polythene sheeting and cover the bottom with fine gravel.

Start off with 100 two-inch trout, which will cost about £5. Take the precaution of covering the pond with fine mesh wire to keep the birds and cats out.

Most Government and commercial fish hatcheries deal exclusively with salmon, trout and sea trout eggs. Growth rates of game fish are shown in the graph (B).

friendly lot of people, coming from every walk of life and background. It is rare indeed to find one who won't spend time helping and advising a beginner and showing him the rudiments of casting. You need only wander round a reservoir bank till you see someone casting well, and then ask him if he can spare a few minutes to advise you. The probability is that he will cheerfully help you as much as he can.

Fly casting is a very pleasant exercise even if you're not catching fish, which is one reason why trout fishing is so popular. Another is that you don't have to carry nearly so much equipment as the sea-fisher or coarse-fish angler, nor be involved in the preparation of baits, some of which are rather messy or smelly.

There is also the pleasure of collecting artificial flies, many of which are objets d'art. If you are wise, you will soon learn to make your own. There are plenty of anglers who will show you how, and in some areas fly-tying classes are held. It is much more satisfying to catch a trout on a fly you made

Teach-In on WORMHOLES

TO KEEP an all-the-year-round supply of worms, which are still the best bait, just dig a hole in a shady part of the garden (Picture A) and stick a drainpipe in the centre. Pack the base of the hole with old sacking and compost, and keep it damp by feeding a cupful of milk down the pipe.

Start off your supply of worms by gathering lobworms at night from lawns, bowling greens and cricket pitches. Lug-worms and ragworms for sea fishing will keep for several days if they are separated and packed in layers of newspaper and lightly covered with earth.

Be careful when fishing rivers that are in spate. Picture B1 shows the deep and dangerous holes that get covered (as in B2) when the rains come. At low tide, probe a metal 'cleek' into half-covered rock crevices. Lurking lobsters and crabs will take hold of the hook and they can then be pulled out.

AIDS TO TROUT ANGLING.

GORDON

TEACH-IN: Get that raft ready for action!

THE LINE RAFT (Pictures A and B) is 15 inches across, and it can be folded for packing. The nylon netting is press-studded to the rim. Holes on the outside make it easier to tie the raft to a wader strap or to anchor it on the bottom. The Tray (C) has hook-on tabs, and it fits snugly to the body. Both sides should be of sombre colour. Olive green is best – it doesn't scare the fish.

The first mad rush of a hooked trout can be unexpected and alarming. If the loose coils of line catch on a clothing button or a boot strap, the sudden jerk snaps the nylon leader and the fish goes free. Modern smooth tapered lines shoot further and easier. When reservoir fishing, 30 to 40 yards of line are often in use as each cast is retrieved.

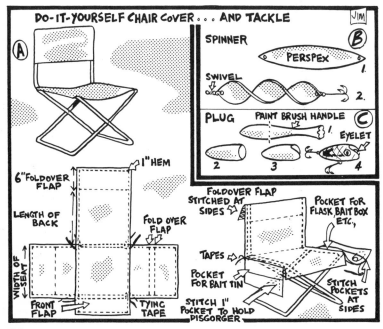

DO-IT-YOURSELF CHAIR COVER . . . AND TACKLE   JIM

Ⓐ

1" HEM

6" FOLDOVER FLAP

LENGTH OF BACK

FOLD OVER FLAP

WIDTH OF SEAT

FRONT FLAP

TYING TAPE

SPINNER   Ⓑ
PERSPEX   1.
SWIVEL   2.

PLUG   PAINT BRUSH HANDLE   Ⓒ
                          1. EYELET
2   3   4

FOLDOVER FLAP STITCHED AT SIDES

POCKET FOR FLASK, BAIT BOX ETC.,

TAPES

POCKET FOR BAIT TIN

STITCH 1" POCKET TO HOLD DISGORGER

STITCH POCKETS AT SIDES

Teach-In on gear

OUT in all sorts of weather, the anglers' chair rarely lasts for more than one season. But its life can be prolonged with strong canvas or carpet (Picture A) and it can be glued or stitched. If a stool is used, just leave off the back part.

Make old-fashioned but very effective spinners (B) from strips of coloured and clear perspex about 1½ins wide. After shaping and heating the perspex, twist it by using a pair of pliers at each end.

Pike and salmon plugs made from old paintbrush handles (C) will again save you money.

yourself than on a shop-bought one, and even more satisfying if you not only made but also invented the fly instead of copying someone else's pattern. Fly-tying is a hobby within a hobby – and making your own flies saves you a lot of expense, too.

Now let's talk about the trout. He bears much the same relationship to other freshwater fish as the hawk or falcon does to other birds. He's a dashing, swashbuckling sort of fellow, but he can be fussy at times about what he wants to eat. Sometimes he will dash at almost any fly you offer him if he doesn't see you first, but at other times he wants an imitation of some special species of insect that happens to be hatching out. If you haven't got one, and can't sit down on the bank and make one, you won't catch him and that's that!

Having the right fly isn't everything. You have to offer him that fly just right, so that it behaves like the real insect does. Because different kinds of insects behave in different ways, there's a lot to learn, and

the observant chap who watches everything he sees at the waterside scores heavily over the man who decides which fly to fish, and how to fish it, before he arrives at the waterside.

Sometimes our dashing friend the trout goes all coy. He comes up and takes a close look at our fly, and then says, or seems to say: 'No, thanks, you'll have to do better than that if you want to catch me!' That sort of behaviour produces a greatly accelerated pulse rate in the angler, though not to the same extent as when the trout seizes the fly, you tighten, and in three seconds 40 yards of line has gone screaming off your reel and Mr Trout is three feet up in the air, in the middle of a rainbow halo of water drops and spray. It's then that your heartbeat really speeds up and your knees tremble.

Sometimes the trout eats things too small to imitate, like daphnia and tiny midge flies, and then the fishing is frustrating. Sometimes, especially on big waters and in hot weather, all the trout are 30ft

TEACH-IN on the FLY FAMILY

THE ANGLER in our picture is on a typical chalkstream fly-water. He is fishing upstream to a selected trout which has been 'dimpling'. The dry fly cannot sink. It floats on the surface, down to the waiting fish.

Artificial flies catch more anglers than fish, but all of the artificials are based upon the live insect. The various patterns and types of dressing are numberless. And new ones come out regularly. Identification of the natural fly is easy – they come into four distinct winged groups:

Picture A shows the flat-winged fly. In shape it resembles the common housefly. B shows a fly with soft, hairy wings lying along the body in a roof shape. C is the upwinged fly, with a segmented body and two or three tails. D is the long, narrow, hard-winged fly. Some members of this family cannot take flight.

All fish get more protein from a diet of flies than they do from any other form of wild feeding.

down and you have to use a fast-sinking line and time its descent through the water with a stop watch, trying different sinking times till you catch a fish and learn what sinking time to allow to catch others. Sometimes you have to call on all your casting ability to drive a fly into a strong headwind; sometimes you're out in a boat in a flat calm, seeing rising fish all around, but none within casting range. You wait patiently hoping that one will move within reach.

Or you may be out in a strong wind and big waves, your catch depending more on your boat-handling than your ability as an angler. The boat goes up and down like a yo-yo, tackle handling is difficult, when you hook a fish it's hard to keep the line taut, and you lose a few as well as catching some, for that reason.

Then there's the river, perhaps in mayfly time,

when big mayflies with a wing span of nearly 1½ins are floating down in droves. You see fish coming up and taking them, but you say to yourself: 'No, I won't try for the first fish I see. I'll walk quietly up the river till I see an extra big fish feeding, and try for him!'

So you do eventually find such a fish, obviously a five-pounder, chomping every fly that comes down the current and making no end of a disturbance. You go down on all fours and creep up to within casting range, hiding as best you can behind two thistles and a stem of willow herb. You may find too late that a cow has passed that way before you, or a moorhen that was hiding under the bank may scutter across the water, treading on the trout's head and scaring him stiff for the next hour. But you may be more fortunate and avoid such handicaps. You extend your line, drop your float upstream of the fish. It floats down to him. He ignores it. You try again, with the same results. So you take off your fly and try another mayfly pattern.

Six fly-changes later, you realise the fish is craftier than you expected. You tie on an emergency mayfly, one with some orange feather in it, quite unlike any real mayfly. You cast. The fish takes the fly, you tighten, he rushes downstream, leaving your line slack, but not for long. You're up and running after him, reel screeching, as fast as you can go. He dives under a fallen tree branch, there's a jar, the line goes slack and you reel up with shaking hands to find the fly is missing.

You go to a big reservoir like Grafham or Chew Valley. Nothing can be seen feeding at the surface, so you fix up your light but powerful reservoir fly rod, with a fast sinking line, at the end of which is a stout nylon leader. You put on a big, fancy fly that resembles no insect that ever crawled or flew. It's made of goat hair and if it looks like anything at all, it gives the impression of a little fish when it is pulled through the water. You wade out as far as your thigh-boots allow and begin casting. You've learned the double-haul casting style, the kind the tournament casters use, with your left hand moving the line in exact synchronisation with the right hand moving the rod. That greatly increases your casting range, and it is fun to see your line streaking out 40 yards or more.

After each cast, you retrieve, pulling line through the rod rings and dropping it into a mesh-bottomed canvas line basket strapped round your waist, to

Patience is rewarded and a trout is netted at Springlakes, Ash Vale, near Aldershot.

avoid tangles. Yachts are sailing about the reservoir, but you don't worry, for they're being sailed by nice fellows who take care not to trespass on the area where you are fishing. They're pleasant to watch, but if one capsizes you'll move back closer to the bank, for you can expect the wash from the high-speed rescue launch before long.

While you're watching those yachts, retrieving line and trying to make your fly move in darts, like a tiny fish, your mind wanders a little. Just when you're wondering whether those ducks are mallards or tufted ducks, an almighty tug nearly takes the rod out of your hand.

Ten minutes later, you're splashing your way back to the bank with a beautiful rainbow trout in your landing net, and three or four other anglers are coming along the bank to admire it, to congratulate you on the skilful way in which you handled it, and to ask which fly you caught it on. You tell them; you see that one of them hasn't any of that sort, and you give him one of yours, and then he goes and catches a trout just like yours.

Presently, it is time to go home, and the two of you walk back to the car park together, talking fishing, and he tells you the story of the English angler who spent a fortnight in Ireland and caught a trout on the last day, and O'Rafferty the boatman said it was a grand fish, bejasus. And the angler said it damn well ought to be; it had cost £200, what with the air fare, and the hotel, and the boat hire, and all. And O'Rafferty said sure then, 'twas a mercy ye didn't catch another, ye'd never have been able to afford it.

He gets into his car and drives away, and you see the fishery manager and say 'Who's that chap?' and the manager says 'Oh, he's Lord Whoosit,' or 'Oh, he's our milkman' or 'Oh, he's a police superintendent' or whatever, and you reflect on the fact that angling is a sort of freemasonry, and people are all very much alike once they get a fishing rod in their hands.

When you get home and unload your catch, it's not too late to step down the road and give a nice fresh trout to the old couple in No. 23; and nobody says: 'I can't understand why you fishermen catch fish only to throw them back!' Because you don't put trout back. You and your friends can eat them, and very nice they are – much better than the skinny, tasteless little trout you see on the fishmonger's slab at an outrageous price.

There's more, far more, to trout fishing than I've been able to tell you about here. So why don't you find out the rest for yourself? If you do, you'll never regret it.

NOW HERE'S A TOP KNOT TIP

SOME hooks are made with a spade-end. They do not have a loop or eye. These five easy stages show how to go about making a very sure hold and a neatly finished knot.

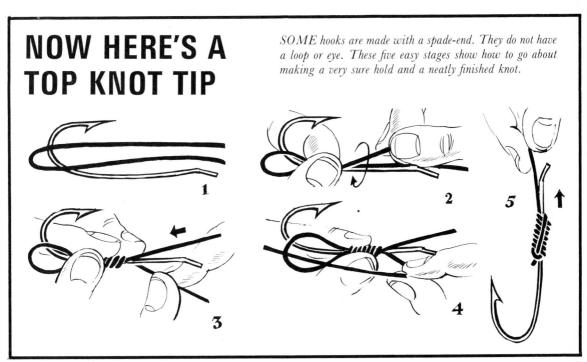

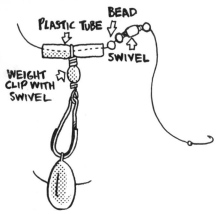

Sliding tackle rigs sometimes fray the line. This can be cured by making a 'cushion' from one-and-a-half inches of hollow plastic tube. The tube must be slightly heated before being forced through the eye of the swivel.

The ugly knot made by a cast connector frightens the fish. So whip the shank of a discarded hook to the end of the fly line and there will be no devastating splash when the line hits the water.

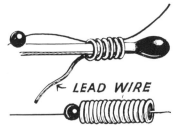

Neat coils of lead wire are so simple when you know how to go about making them. Your total equipment – one matchstick.

Cut off the top half of an empty polythene detergent bottle. Insert a length of cane to serve as a handle and bind the joint with Sellotape. Now you have a maggot thrower which is accurate and which can be used with one hand.

To catch bass and mackerel, wind lead to a long shanked hook and then streamline it with hen feather, and swivel (B). An unweighted feathered lure can also be fished up the line (A).

Rooting out bottom growth and removing floating duckweed beats most fishermen. But the tools shown here make the job simple. 1) The scoop is made from three pieces of 2″ × 1″ board joined at an angle. 2) The rake is adapted from a garden leaf-gatherer. Attach both tools to strong rope and cast them out and then drag back.

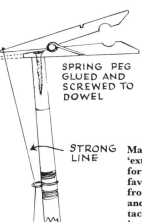

Make yourself an 'extra long arm' for retrieving favourite floats from reed beds and special fly tackle hooked up in the trees.

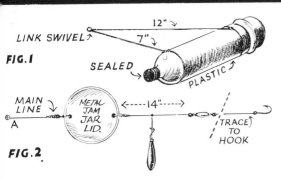

FIG.1

FIG.2

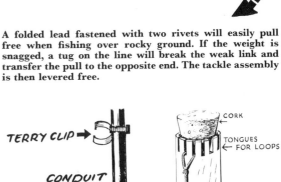

FIGURE 1 shows how to retrieve snagged tackle with a home made 'otter'. To use it, the link swivel is clipped to the line and the action of the current pulls the hook free.

FIGURE 2 is the perfect method of fishing rocky coastlines without losing valuable terminal tackle. The lid of the jam jar aquaplanes and the weight is lifted instantly from the sea bed.

A folded lead fastened with two rivets will easily pull free when fishing over rocky ground. If the weight is snagged, a tug on the line will break the weak link and transfer the pull to the opposite end. The tackle assembly is then levered free.

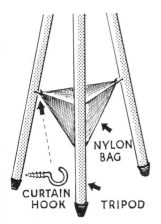

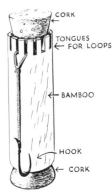

Demolishing old buildings helps to fill scrapyards with lengths of used electric conduit tubing. Salvage some old bits and pieces of the galvanised tubing to make this easily-constructed beach rod stand (diagram on right).

At night the shore-line is dotted with anglers' lamps. But they are usually worn as headgear similar to a miner's lamp. This idea gives both light and heat.

Take a piece of bamboo and glue in two corks. Make the snoods to the hooks slightly shorter than the bamboo-holder and there will be no more tangles with tackle when beach and pier fishing.

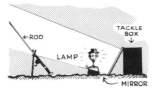

Time is meaningless to a fisherman. The day speeds by and it is dark before he knows it. To keep gear safe, use a white handkerchief marker on the fishing bag – but be sure it is in a place where a big wave will not wash over. Some anglers fit a white nylon bag to a tripod, and it folds up quite easily when the tripod rod rest is packed.

Rivet a tobacco tin to an old wrist watch strap and worms, maggots, shot, etc can always be at hand. Without putting the rod down or coming out of the water, changes can be made. It saves valuable fishing time.

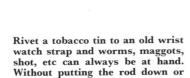

PUNCH HOLES IN LID

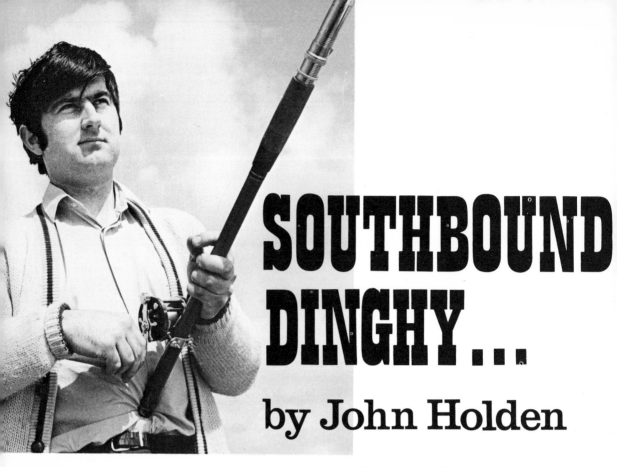

SOUTHBOUND DINGHY...

by John Holden

JOHN HOLDEN was British Amateur Surfcasting Champion of 1969 and 1970 when he was in his early twenties, and was second professional in the 4oz fixed-spool event of the 1973 World Casting Championships. He was one of the first British anglers to cast over 200 yards at a public demonstration. He has cast professionally for F. W. Woolworth and has been concerned in development of Winfield tackle. John is an angling writer/photographer with special interests in sea-fishing, marine biology and the history of commercial fishing. He is a senior technologist in a hospital pathology department.

Gently does it! Scale

CONFINED space makes it dangerous to attempt t
cast the bait out when fishing from a boat (A). Use
short rod and lower the bait gently to the sea bed. Star
with a heavy lead and gradually scale it down to th
correct weight. A light line will tangle with othe
anglers or become wrapped around the boat propelle

WE PUSHED out the dinghy. The early morning was flat and calm. Cold too; ice lacquered the thwarts and bottomboards. John flooded the carburettor and a rainbow of petrol slicked the water. The Seagull fired first pull, coughed, picked up and settled into a reedy staccato. The clutch bit; she answered the helm and headed her bows South. The wake whitened the grey water. Exhaust bubbles popped to the surface and burst into oily steam which drifted away.

Offshore, the sea was still, silky-looking because of the clouds of suspended silt. Herring gulls and clumps of wrack speckled the surface. As we passed, the gulls flew East into the fog-veiled disc of the dawn sun. We were not alone on the sea. Other dinghies rode at anchor. We burbled by, conversing with them in sign language. Someone held up a small cod; head and shoulders emerged from beneath the canvas dodger of a dinghy like ours – thumbs down, nothing yet.

Clear of the land, the groundswell rolled lazily in under our port bow. She buried her head into the bigger swells. Spray slapped up from the bow planks and showered aboard in icy drops. We ran for an hour. Land faded, merged into the sea, and disappeared. The compass rose held steady South.

I switched on the sounder as we approached the sandbanks. The neon flickered round the dial and settled on 25ft 25 . . . 25 . . . 30, 40, 30 . . . 20. John shoved the motor hard over and we came round. Back down to 35 ft. The dinghy ran East now, skirting the sea-bed channel. John turned off the petrol and I made ready with the anchor. The Seagull died and we lost way. The anchor sank down on its long chain and 15 fathoms of rope.

She stopped, and drifted back in the half-flood current. I slipped the rope into the fairlead. Her bows swung straight into the tide. The flukes gripped and slipped, dug in again and held fast.

The rods had been made up back shore. I clipped a 6oz grip lead to the running leger trace. I peeled back the damp newspapers from the heavy bait-box and raked through a mass of big, black lugworms. I threaded four of them up the trace, then pulled them back down in a juicy ball over the 6/0 hook. We cast uptide away from the boat so that the tackle anchored across the tide run. Water pressure stretched the nylon and bent the rod tip over the gunwhales.

The sun moved low along the Southern horizon; the fog lightened into mist. A foghorn sounded downtide echoed by the bass thump of a marine diesel. We peered towards the noise; ours would not have been the first dinghy smashed by a coaster. A deeply-laden timber ship loomed out of the haze and ghosted safely past on the other side of the sands.

My rod flicked straight as the line fell loose. I reeled in the slack and tightened down on a fish which plodded off in the current. Line and fish swung downstream; a few feet of line slipped off against the clutch. But it was not a hard fighting fish – more a deadweight kiting in the tide.

Twenty yards behind the dinghy, a cod splashed to the top. I dragged it open-mouthed and wallowing to the side of the boat. John lifted it over the gunwales in the big landing net. It thudded into the fish-box. A small cod – 10lb at most.

I unskewered the hook from its tongue, rebaited and cast again. John was into his first fish now and I netted it for him. Three cod came quickly. A whiting, too. But as the tide slowed on high water the fish moved away. The anchor rope slackened; the dinghy drifted and twisted in the wind which sprang up with top-water.

The mist cleared and Clacton pier showed in the

B). Most fish will take a jigging spoon (C) which *ints in the water. To avoid line twist, use a swivel nk at the head of the spoon. Tough gloves are vital *hen handling wire traces used for tope, shark and *nger. Spiny fish (D) like bass should be handled *ith great care.

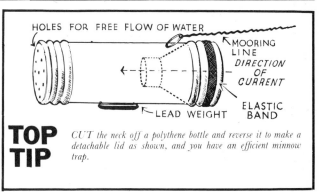

TOP TIP

HOLES FOR FREE FLOW OF WATER

MOORING LINE

DIRECTION OF CURRENT

ELASTIC BAND

LEAD WEIGHT

CUT the neck off a polythene bottle and reverse it to make a detachable lid as shown, and you have an efficient minnow trap.

far distance. We cleaned up the dinghy and ate our sandwiches. I poured a cup of soup from my Thermos and cradled the hot cup in my hands. My fingers absorbed the heat and tingled back to life.

An hour and a half down, the ebb rushed past, funnelling fast and dirty from the Blackwater estuary. The anchor rope vibrated and creaked like a bowstring. Tearing water slapped and chattered under the hull. But the fish came back to feed viciously in the tide. Pulling them up from the bottom and into the boat was hindered by our having to fight the sea as well as the fish. As the sun fell, the wind blew up from under it.

The sea stirred. The waves lopped and lumped. The troughs lengthened; the tops of the waves turned over white and foaming. A bitter East Anglian wind-haze knifed across the water. It was time to go; time to call it a day and cut our losses, for the East Coast is no place for a dinghy when the wind blows.

John braced himself in the stern and refilled the petrol tank. Choke on . . . coil the starting cord . . . pull. She fired. John slipped her into gear and opened the throttle a shade. She crept up the anchor rope, and I hand-over-handed it back aboard.

The dinghy's bows tossed as a big wave caught her. She corkscrewed down into the trough. I whipped in the slack and jammed the rope into the fairlead. The next crest lifted her high, tensed the rope and craned the anchor out of the mud. She drifted free. John held her on the throttle as I pulled in the anchor and chain.

We ploughed back in the failing light. Clouds lowered and a few drops of rain dabbed into our coats. All over the sea, other dinghies made for land; moving carefully, riding out the big following sea; ever watchful for the rogue waves which could bucket in over the stern and kill the engine.

A hundred yards out now; surf pounded the beach. We slowed, let the sea take her. The engine ticked over just fast enough to give her steerage way. Thirty yards. A big green sea swept under the stern. John opened the throttle wide. She surged in, surfing on the hump of dark water. The wave broke and we hit the beach in a carpet of surf and spray. I jumped out. Accustomed to the dinghy's pitch and roll, my legs felt rubbery on the hard sand.

The other crews helped manhandle the dinghy to the trailer, through the soft sand, up the slipway and to the van. In turn, we helped them recover their boats. It seems to have been a reasonable day, everyone agreed. Not like the old days, of course. But not bad.

I went down to the sea and gutted the cod, packing them neatly into the fish-box. Cleaned and washed, the catch weighed about 50lb. I carried the box to where John waited in the van. And the herring gulls came in from the twilight to squabble in the surf for the leftovers.

TEACH-IN on wrecks, buoys and the weather

SEA-ANGLING craft (Picture A) should be at least 12ft in length. And the safe rule is to carry no more than two anglers in a 12ft boat, three anglers in a 14ft boat and four anglers in a 16-footer.

Take proper notice of the wind and weather, radio forecasts (B) and learn the 'rules of the road' and what the various shaped buoys (C) stand for. Leave to starboard the conical shaped buoys 1, 2 and 3 – and leave to port the can-shaped buoys 4, 5, 6.

Wreck markings (D) with three vertical flashing green lights should be left to starboard. Those with two flashing green lights should be left to port.

When overtaking (E), keep out of the way of the other vessels.

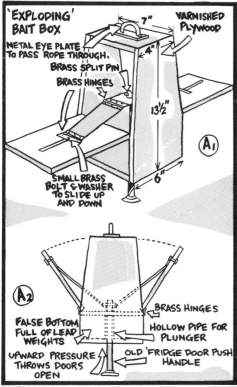

'EXPLODING' BAIT BOX

VARNISHED PLYWOOD

METAL EYE PLATE TO PASS ROPE THROUGH.

BRASS SPLIT PIN

BRASS HINGES

7"

4"

13½"

6"

Ⓐ₁

SMALL BRASS BOLT & WASHER TO SLIDE UP AND DOWN

Ⓐ₂

BRASS HINGES

FALSE BOTTOM FULL OF LEAD WEIGHTS

HOLLOW PIPE FOR PLUNGER

UPWARD PRESSURE THROWS DOORS OPEN

OLD 'FRIDGE DOOR PUSH HANDLE

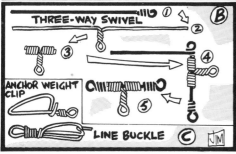

THREE-WAY SWIVEL

① ② ③ ④ ⑤

Ⓑ

ANCHOR WEIGHT CLIP

LINE BUCKLE

Ⓒ

JM

Exploding a bright idea

FRESHWATER anglers, with their sophisticated groundbaiting methods and bait-droppers designed to attract fish, were the envy of Wessex sea angling club member Peter Taylor. So he designed a bait-dropper for sea fishermen and he called it the exploding bait box (Picture A).

The box is filled with crushed mussels, prawns, offal, fish heads and fresh bait. And the weights in the false bottom push up the plunger to open the doors and release the groundbait which brings fish milling around.

In Picture B, angler R. J. Lloyd (Swansea) shows how to make sea swivels, buckles and clips from scraps of wire. He says: 'Fine welding wire is best.'

But before starting to make the tackle and to make the wire easier to handle, it is necessary to use a jig which is easily made from a 12in square piece of wood with round nails hammered in about an inch apart – and then cut the heads of the nails.

TEACH-IN on Nets

ROD ANGLERS fish for sport, but commercial fishermen do it for a livelihood. Various types of net (see illustrations) are used by commercial fishermen to catch salmon and sea trout. With one sweep of the net it is possible to take more salmon than 100 rods can catch in a whole season.

Coracle nets and seine-type nets are operated in the rivers, and the T-shaped net is strung out from the shore and tended from a boat. They are all quite legal and licensed.

On the high seas, finely-meshed nylon nets which are light and practically invisible to the fish quite often cut into the salmon like a razor blade. The salmon and sea trout which hit the net or manage to escape from it are often left with severe abrasions.

Anglers who do come across salmon or other freshwater fish with abrasions and damaged scales should report the matter to the Ministry of Agriculture, Fish and Food, who are seeking to stem diseases in fish.

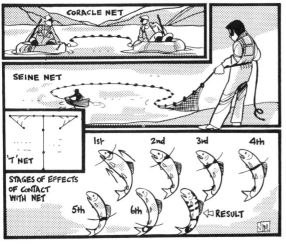

CORACLE NET

SEINE NET

'T' NET

STAGES OF EFFECTS OF CONTACT WITH NET

1st 2nd 3rd 4th

5th 6th RESULT

JM

Somewhere

'*There is no better place to be involved in this fine sport than in Britain, with her vast multiplicity of rivers, lakes, streams and reservoirs...*'

By FRANK GODSMAN

IT IS a long hop, even by Concorde, from the steaming jungles of Zaire (known as the Belgian Congo in the days I fished there) to the peaceful banks of the Test in Hampshire. It is an even longer hop from the broad, sun-warmed Vaal River in the Transvaal to the green, expansive banks of the Tweed in Berwickshire.

To the experienced angler, however, the 'jump' is not all that bewildering or frustrating: it merely entails a change of locale and species. Give him a hint on the food and habits of the species he is hunting and in no time he'll have a fish or two on the business end of his tackle – if, that is, he's worthy of the name 'fisherman'.

Most of my early fishing was done in the Vaal and Klip Rivers in South Africa at Vereeniging, and on Vaaldam, that large man-made lake where Solent flying-boats came to rest on flights from Britain.

Memories flood back of those early days ... lightning forking out of purple storm-clouds on hot summer afternoons as the bait – a dead dove, frog or

chicken entrails on a large hook – landed with a splash on the glassy surface of a dam ... a swirl and the bait would be taken by a barbel with a maw the size of a bulldog's ... at day's end, carrying from the riverside to the car the catch in a sack that two of us could hardly lift ... and the wide, joyful grins of the Africans as they tipped the barbel into a hole in the ground lined with eucalyptus leaves that were set alight, eventually to yield succulent, baked fish.

And still, in almost total recall, the memorable tropical days return, as years later and more than a thousand miles north of the Transvaal, up in central Africa, one paddled a dugout, hewn out of a log, on clean pale-green waters where exotic birds cried out as they fluttered in gaudy plumage between the tall trees towering above the banks of the river.

The waters, in sparkling, unpolluted torrents, tumbled over the rocks at Kapalala Falls. The Africans, motivated by hunger rather than by any sporting instinct, built a crude barrier of branches across a narrow section of the boiling rapids. They left a 10ft gap through which the tigerfish and

the sun is shining...

FRANK GODSMAN was born in Durban, South Africa. He followed careers as metallurgist and aeronautical draughtsman until the printer's ink in his blood, inherited from his Scottish journalist father, induced him into newspaper and periodical journalism. He was the founding editor of several specialist magazines in Northern Rhodesia (now Zambia) before settling in Britain, where he works at 'the most fascinating job of all' – editor of *Fisherman* magazine.

Editor of 'Fisherman'

bream would have to pass on their way downstream. The sleek tigerfish, speckled with black markings, slid through and at once found themselves trapped in a small natural pool formed by a ring of boulders.

In this pool a pair of sturdy young African tribesmen pranced about, jabbing at the 'tigers' with sharpened stakes. The men impaled the fish and swung them over on to a flat shelf of rock. Soon scores of beautiful silvery bodies flapped their black-and-orange tails in anguish, and finally lay still. At cerise sundown, the chief arrived to distribute the catch among the heads of the tribal families. They quickly departed to make a meal of the tigerfish, whose bodies were extremely bony though the flesh was sweet and delicious.

We 'sporting anglers' set forth in dugouts and paddled to the shallows below the rapids. Here among the half-submerged rocks lurked the notorious tigerfish, lying in wait for passing shoals of bream or tilapia, a small indigenous fish.

We trolled spinners, plugs or deadbait attached to treble hooks. So aggressive were the tigerfish that they would launch themselves at almost anything that moved – even beer-bottle tops skimming across the surface!

Nor is it for meekness that the tigerfish (*Hydrocynus or water dog*) have gained a reputation as the greatest sporting fish in the world. They hit the lure at incredible speeds and zoom off downstream, stripping off 50yd to 100yd of line from the reel almost before one has had time to steady the dugout. (It was quite a feat to play one of those sabre-toothed 'fliers' and, at the same time, to maintain one's balance in the narrow dugout!)

Once the tigerfish turned and leaped out of the water, one had to keep the line taut between rod-tip and quarry. The tigerfish has an impressive head: its jaws are massive, and the upper one is hinged so that it can swing upwards, the teeth pointed forward, in readiness to snap shut on its prey. The skin is stretched over the bony frame like parchment. Once airborne in a 6ft vertical leap, it twists its powerful, spindle-shaped body and savagely shakes its head in attempts to throw the hook.

One had to be wary, even after a long struggle, as the 'tiger' came alongside the dugout, or near the river-bank. The moment it caught sight of its adversary it often gave a final wild leap into the air. It would give a desperate headshake, or swerve off around a rock, so powerfully that it could straighten a large single hook. They fought gamely right to the end, so that it was imperative, the moment a 'tiger' was aboard the dugout, to crack it on the head with a heavy spanner or stout bit of wood. Failure to do so could mean a chunk missing from one's haunch – or worse.

All good primitive stuff, you may think, and then wonder: But how does the fishing in the British Isles compare with that on the African scene?

For one thing, Britain has a far greater variety of

species of fish and a wealth of stocked water. Then again, the compactness of the British Isles enables the angler to reach a river, natural lake, stocked reservoir, gravel-pit, canal or chalk-stream without having to undertake a minor safari.

Besides the easy access and availability, the splendid variety of coarse, sea and game fish and waters gives the British angler the opportunity to master more techniques than his counterpart in less fortunate countries, and consequently he can fish throughout the year. He is, in fact, in a most enviable position, and it is no wonder that angling is Britain's largest participant sport.

The 'explosion' of angling in this country, in particular during the past few years, has created certain problems. Not the least of these is to satisfy the growing demand for fishing space. Sailing, boating, canoeing and other aquatic sports are creating additional pressure on water resources.

The problem of shrinking waters and rising demand cannot, of course, be solved by creating new rivers and streams. But valuable substitutes have been produced and they are constantly being increased. The Leisure Sport organisation, for instance, has developed many stocked gravel-pits, and it has plans for laying out attractive water-parks

Secrets of fly dressing

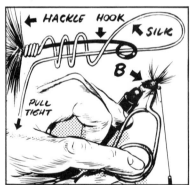
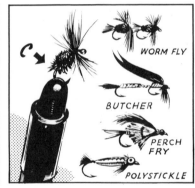

THE HARDEST part of fly dressing is in getting the hackles correct. Drawing A shows that by taking a few turns of the silk in front of the hackle, the secret is solved.

Drawing B shows the trimming and tying-in of the hackle. The final operation is the whip-finish; everything must be tight.

Drawing C, if you haven't already guessed, is the artificial fly we have been working on – the black-and-peacock spider. The fly is very successful on lake and reservoir.

Tinsel in strips from a milk-bottle top makes a silver or golden variation for the ribbing. The added weight of the foil will also allow the fly to fish just under the surface, as in nymphing.

Worm flies sometimes operate best for sea trout if a small

spinner is mounted at the head. The butchers tied in tandem are acceptable offerings to large lake trout in coloured water or at night.

Perch fry and polystickles have come into favour recently. Purist anglers argue that they are not flies, but imitation small fish. Both viewpoints are correct. Using a fly rod and keeping the lure on the move, retrieve in small twitches; when the fish takes, the action is no different from wet fly fishing.

Some fly-tyers earn a living at the bench and never fish; they are happy with pretty creations. But the angler who goes to the water and presents to the trout a self-made fly which is accepted, is cock-a-hoop.

which, among many amenities, will eventually include waters set aside for fly-fishermen.

Abstraction is playing hell with some rivers. Encroaching concrete structures and thirsty factories, sucking up water and spewing it out again in a vile mess of filth and chemicals, present further problems.

The effects of pollution on the waters of this green and glorious land are too well known to be harped on here. But the types of pollution are becoming extensive and more insidious. A serious situation has arisen of acid rainfall over Scandinavia owing to sulphur dioxide emissions from the industrial complexes of Europe, including Britain. This acid rainfall is already affecting the productivity of freshwater lakes in Norway and Sweden. The development of North Sea oil, and the rigs and pipe-lines off Scotland, present yet another new set of pollution problems.

Over-fishing and pollution are decimating the noble salmon. In England and Wales the salmon runs are at an all-time low, and even in Scotland they have shown an alarming drop in the past century.

It would be presumptuous of me, as a comparative newcomer to the British angling scene, and without benefit of considerable research, to suggest how the dwindling salmon population of the country could be restored. But Anthony Netboy, lecturer on salmon conservation and retired Professor of English in the Oregon State System of

TEACH-IN on Lines

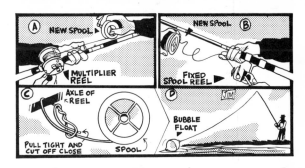

ALTHOUGH nylon line does not rot and can be said to be almost everlasting, the line does get weak when twisted and tight knots will reduce its strength by as much as 25 per cent. It is good policy to buy a new line now and again.

Picture A shows how to fit a new line to a multiplier reel. The new spool and the reel rotate in the same direction and the line goes on without twisting. With a fixed-spool reel (B), the new line holder should face the front of the reel to allow the line to flow without twisting.

A neat strong knot (C) should always be used when loading a new line to the reel. If during a day's fishing the line develops a bad twist, it can be rectified by letting all the line out on a bubble float and re-winding (D). It can also be let out in a field.

TEACH-IN on moving and flashing baits

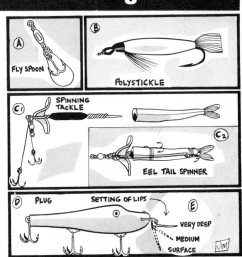

ALL FISH are gangsters. They snap at, and seek to destroy, weaker fish. Invariably the marauding fish is attracted to a moving bait which flashes in the water. Trout, salmon, pike, roach and dace will go for the fly spoon (Picture A). The oval-shaped spoon is coloured silver on one side and copper on the other, and it rotates around the tiny double-hook.

The polystickle (B) resembles a minnow, and it is constructed from raffia and polythene wrapped around a silvered hook. A favourite bait (C) for big salmon is a sand-eel tail which is pushed on to a metal-bodied lure.

Plugs (D) have a brightly-painted wood body with very sharp hooks. Sometimes the body is jointed and its erratic movement through the water attracts predatory fish. The lip of the plug is adjustable for making the lure operate at various depths.

Higher Education, has stressed the urgent need of a many-pronged attack.

He summed it up in four general areas: (1) Cleaning up some of the better salmon rivers so that more fish can live in them; (2) building of large-scale hatcheries to raise salmon to the smolt stage; (3) a research programme to provide knowledge necessary for restoring the runs and their management; (4) improved management of the rivers for the benefit of the fisheries.

The Regional Water Authorities inherited the duties of the river authorities after the Water Act of 1973, and the steps they are taking are showing results. It was heartening to learn, in November 1974, for instance, of the 'One-in-a-million-pound fish' – the celebrated salmon that was found in the wire screens of West Thurrock power station. The fish was proclaimed as heralding a new era in the Thames Water Authority's fight against pollution in the river. With the discovery of the salmon, 73 species of fish were now known to inhabit the river.

There is genuine concern about the problems but, fundamentally, it is the community's responsibility and not alone the angler's to decide what the future will be.

I find it gratifying that, although I have not made fishing *per se* a way of life, at least I have been able to make a living through a close facet of it – angling journalism. Few other branches of journalism in which I have been engaged are so satisfying or fascinating. There is no better place to be involved in this fine sport than in Britain, with her vast multiplicity of rivers, lakes, streams and reservoirs.

What a pity it is that so many of us take these waters for granted.

The FISH that builds a HOUSE

PLUCKY little sticklebacks, so common in our ponds and streams, are among the few breeds of fish which make a nest for the protection of their eggs.

In the picture (bottom right), the male is busily collecting weeds and stalks as building material. In the centre, the female disappears inside the nest to lay. The water is alive with small sticklebacks in the spring, but at other times of the year they successfully hide away.

When breeding, all males have brilliant red flanks and underbelly; the female fish is a drab yellow with greenish back.

Water scorpions (detailed, top left) are the recluses of the insect world. Able to stay underwater for long periods, they prey on little fishes.

For some unknown reason, the trout will fall for a stickleback bait more readily than for the inoffensive and smoother minnow.

NOTHING in the world will prevent anglers from losing tackle. Rocks, weeds and underwater tree roots are ever-present but hidden hazards. To cut losses to a minimum, use the rig shown in the top left picture.

Sea fishermen will also find the method useful when fishing over soft mud, where the bait gets buried. Or because the bait lies where small crabs can steal it before the fish get a chance even to inspect the offering.

Sand crabs always cease their marauding as darkness falls. So anglers, especially those after whiting and fishing from the shore, should wait until dusk before tackling up.

Saving your tackle

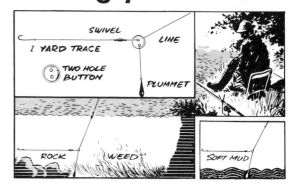

They love those tattered flies

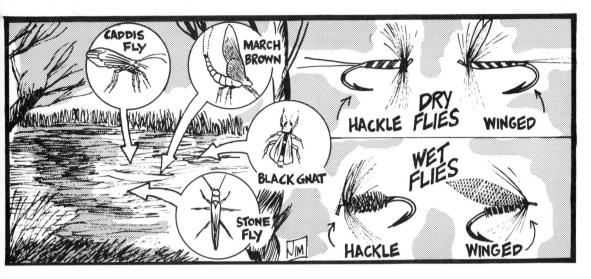

ARTIFICIAL flies are meant to resemble the real insects, but more anglers get hooked by the prettily-coloured tinsel flies than fish. The more tattered and bedraggled the fly becomes, the more appealing and natural it is.

When the insects (left of picture) hatch out, the hungry trout and dace have a real binge of frenzied feeding. A diet of insects will fatten a fish faster than a diet of worms, bread or minnows.

The artificial fly can be fished sunk (which is wet fly) or on the surface (dry fly). A rippling wind over the water makes it easier to deceive the fish.

Flies (right of picture) come in all shapes, sizes and colours. The most important thing is to keep the hook points sharp, and always have an artificial fly to match whatever insect is hatching at the time.

HOOKS

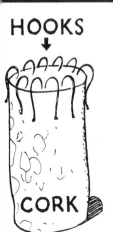

CORK

◀ TRY THIS CORK TIP

Fasten your hooks around one end (or both ends if you like) of an ordinary cork. This saves you fiddling with wet cold hands into tins and soggy envelopes.

MATCH STICK

◀ AND THIS MATCH TIP

To stop the split shot from fouling the hook, knot a matchstick on to the line. It also serves to hold the leger tight and makes 'striking' easier.

NICE ONE, JOHN!

This well-conditioned perch taken on a livebait rig by John Probert scaled 3¼lb.

Plenty of Homework

That's the secret of good perch fishing, says JOHN PROBERT

JOHN PROBERT is a tackle dealer, angling writer and successful big fish catcher. He made his name in the late 'sixties with some tremendous catches of carp, together with his fishing partner Gerry Savage. Now he concentrates on perch and has had several outstanding hauls recently. John is a Kentish man and lives at Erith.

INSTANTLY recognisable by its spiny dorsal fin and vertical stripes, the perch is one of our most colourful and sporting freshwater fishes. Like many anglers I cut my teeth on small perch, and before the mystery killer disease which decimated stocks in the 1960s, the gregarious young perch were normally the first conquest by any newcomer to the sport.

Indeed, with the summer sun at its hottest, when even the roach and rudd lose interest in the angler's titbits, the bold young stripeys queue for any offerings of maggots or worms.

But during the last decade, perch have been notably absent from the vast majority of our lakes and rivers, the only exception being a few isolated venues, most of which contain brackish water. Happily though, the last few years have seen a big comeback in perch stocks and the vast majority of waters, especially my own haunts in the South-East, now contain a good head of young perch. And if this latest welcome trend is anything to go by, we could be in for a really plentiful period of perch sport as, fishery by fishery, the species re-establishes itself.

Perch in the specimen class are really worth pursuing, for unlike their younger brothers, the bigger fish develop an uncanny knack of avoiding the anglers hookbait. If you're lucky enough to know of a water containing big perch, it's well worth putting in plenty of homework before baiting a hook.

Gerry Savage and I gained access to just such a water a few seasons back and we started our assault long before June 16. Conflicting reports led us to believe that the fishery – a disused quarry – was up to 50ft deep in the middle with greatly differing contours over its whole area.

Unable to substantiate or disprove this theory, we decided to borrow a small boat and set to work

FINS and FACES

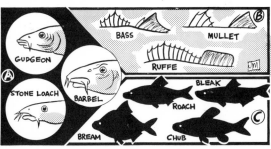

ALL FISH have fascinating faces and shapes. In Picture A, the gudgeon has keen nostrils and a sharp eye. The loach and barbel have beards that act as feelers for seeking out food. Some fish (B) have spiked fins along the top of the back. The points are quite sharp and act as a deterrent to enemies.

Shapes of fish (C) largely depend on where the fish lives and upon how active it is in seeking its food. Leisurely feeders are round and stubby, but the athletic feeders are streamlined and torpedo-shaped.

plotting the whole lake area with an echo sounder. It took only a matter of hours to disprove the mythical depth theories and when we pulled the boat out of the water we had a complete picture of the shallows, bars and deeper holes.

Since then we have found the information gained in that profitable and, incidentally, very enjoyable afternoon to be some of the most useful water lore we've been able to capitalise on at the venue. During that particular season we netted 13 perch over 2lb, with the best weighing in at 3½lb.

On the face of it perch fishing does not offer any more possibilities for variation of methods than any other species but, in fact, being a predatory fish opens up a complete dossier of methods for spinning, livebait and deadbait fishing.

To take deadbaiting as an example, the vast majority of books don't even mention the method. To be perfectly honest, when I first tried it I did wonder if, in fact, I was wasting my time. But, like so often when you hit on a winner, that method caught me a 3lb perch within hours of first using it.

Generally speaking, though, Gerry and I have caught most of our big perch on livebaits. The best five, fish of 4¾lb, 4lb 6oz, 4¼lb, 3½lb and 3¾lb, all fell to the method. And, incidentally, it's an interesting point that the vast majority of our best perch was taken during the lunchtime period and, in particular, between 11am and 2pm.

But back to tactics, and in particular the paternostered livebait, which has proved so successful on the water I mentioned earlier. I've always liked a paternoster rig for both perch and pike livebaiting because it enables the bait to be fished extremely close to reeds or other cover and yet keeps the fish from becoming snagged up.

As a variation, use a surface-seeking bait such as a rudd and let it work near the top. Perch can often be spotted chasing fish in this area and I'm sure a large percentage of their live food is taken well above mid-water. Big perch tend to patrol for their food, and as an additional attraction feed the swim with loose maggots or groundbait so as to hold a large shoal of small fish.

When perch aren't showing themselves on the surface, and particularly in winter, legered lobworms can be a deadly bait. Try the known hotspots from which you know perch have been taken, but also look for new areas such as deep holes or where shoals of small fish tend to congregate.

With the exception of deadbaiting, the methods already discussed are long proven ones and, in many ways, are best suited to stationary fishing. More and more though, with pike as well as perch, I'm finding that roving tactics can be far more productive. Catching perch on spinners can be really exciting and I had a couple of particularly enjoyable days catching fish to around 2lb on spinners earlier in the season.

When you're buying a new rod....

FIT it up in the shop and, playing the tip on the ceiling, push the rod upwards. A good match rod of 12ft and over will flex at the tip only (A) because it is designed for quick hooking and extreme speed at the strike.

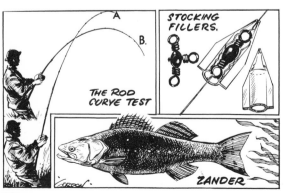

THE ROD CURVE TEST

STOCKING FILLERS.

ZANDER

Leger fishing rods as used for carp and pike are powerful and can land a heavy and strong fighting fish. The curve (B) is progressive from tip to butt.

Swivels are useful stocking fillers at Christmas. The best ones for coarse fishermen are barrel three-way (illustrated). For sea anglers, a few swivel guards will not come amiss. Internal ribs lock over the ring and prevent line twist.

Zander have recently been introduced from eastern Europe to East Anglia rivers. It was a gift that anglers did not ask for, and certainly one which many do not want.

It is neither a pike nor a perch, but it does have the worst habits of both predatory fish. Near Peterborough, a Fen water has fallen entirely to this Mafia fish. Other forms of fish life have been driven out by the usurper.

But as far as the waters I fish are concerned, I'm sure the biggest potential of all for catching big perch consistently lies in slow retrieved deadbaits, either mounted on a very delicate flight or alternatively just lip-hooked with a single hook.

In addition to natural deadbaits, such as roach, rudd, gudgeon, etc, sprats are a good bet and, as with most species, I like them as fresh as possible. There's certainly no need to retrieve the baits quickly and I've found the most successful way is just to inch them erratically, varying the depth at which they are working. A terrific area of water can be covered in this way and, as well as finding it far more enjoyable, it definitely increases the number of perch on the bank.

I mentioned earlier that perch were making a big comeback and generally speaking, I'm sure stocks are better than many anglers would have us believe. Only recently I photographed a 3lb perch from a water supposedly denuded of the species, and can't help but notice the increasing number of specimens reported in the angling Press.

Yes, perch fishing is definitely regaining popularity and it's a trend likely to gather momentum, for once you've sampled the colourful sport of perch fishing you're bound to come back for more.

TEACH-IN on moving fish

GOOD anglers will spend as much time and gain as much pleasure from putting fish into a river as they do in catching them.

When fish stocks from commercial hatcheries are brought long distances, special wagons have to be used. And oxygen is constantly filtered through the carrying tanks to keep the fish happy (Picture A).

A one-wheeled trek cart (B) is useful for carrying nets, fish containers and other heavy equipment along the river bank where narrow plank bridges have to be negotiated. In other places, a carrying stretcher (C) is handy.

When stock fish are transferred from one water to another, the change of temperature has a harmful effect and sometimes fish take days to recover and up to three weeks before feeding.

To minimise shock, the bath or dustbin (with perforated lid removed) is lowered gently into the water and as the river mingles with the carrying water (D), the fish will swim free in their own time.

TEAM SPIRIT!

That's what makes league fishing so appealing

SAYS **BILL HOWES**

BILL HOWES has been an active angler for nearly 40 years. In recent years he has represented England in International Sea Angling Championships. Bill, a professional journalist, is author of 14 books and guides on fishing. As a photographer of the sport, he has built up a library of some 40,000 pictures of angling and allied subjects. He is President of the Surrey Winter League and of the Group 3 Association, Vice-President of Englefield Green AA, Life member of NAC, Associate member of the Zoological Society, member of ACA and a Standing Committee member of the NFSA.

A FAST-GROWING branch of angling is certainly within the field of competition; this is league fishing and it is gaining more followers than the open match circuit. League fishing means club team competition, and working together as a team seems to appeal to more anglers than that of the loner competing in an individual event.

Leagues vary, but without doubt the *Angling Times* League is the biggest with 28 divisions throughout England and Wales. Each division is made up of ten or 12 club teams, with 12 anglers to a team. This means some 4,000-odd anglers are involved. This league has been running for many years and sets the pattern for other leagues.

Teams within a league division compete against

each other over six rounds. The winners of each of
the divisions then compete in nine regional finals,
and the nine winning teams then compete in a
grand final.

Operating throughout the country are winter
leagues, summer leagues, Saturday leagues, evening
leagues, county and inter-area leagues and so on.

Competitors in summer leagues often have boats
and holiday crowds to contend with, but winter
league competition can be really tough. Sometimes
conditions are at their poorest with floods, sharp
frost or snow and ice, and at the best just rain. Yet
however atrocious the conditions, the anglers would
never let their teammates down by not turning up.

Although leagues operate in similar fashion, there
are different ways of arriving at a result. Whichever
system is employed, it is based on the catching of
fish. A man's catch represents either weight or
points, and in some leagues both. A competitor's
position on the result sheet depends on the weight of
his catch, and in some leagues there are points
awarded according to that individual angler's position. As an example, with ten teams of 12 anglers
the match venue is split into ten sections of 12 numbered swims, and team captains draw 'out of the
hat' for peg numbers.

A fair and popular system is that all members of a
particular team fish at the same peg number, from
one to 12 in each section. For instance, if the cap-
tain of team X draws No. 2, then each member of
his team will fish at pegs numbered 2 in each of the
sections. With this system, each section really
becomes its own match with its individual winner.
The man catching the heaviest weight of fish takes
maximum points – say, 10 – the second man nine
points, third eight and so on.

Should a team be on good enough form to
provide the winner of each section they would ac-
cumulate 100 points. Then, as a round-winning
team, they would be awarded ten points in the
league table. Thus, it is possible for a highly successful team to win each of the six rounds and top the
league table with a full 60 points.

Obviously, some leagues are run purely on a
weight-of-fish-caught basis, and as the contest pro-
gresses throughout each round a team's aggregate

*The best-equipped league angler has his box of
special floats.*

weight determines the position it occupies in the
league table.

Venues have much to do with the way a league is
run. For instance, in some parts of the country, particularly in the Midlands, venues are big enough to
accommodate a large number of anglers so that
competing clubs field as many anglers as possible,
perhaps 35 or 40 men. In this case it is the weight of
fish caught by the top 12 men of each club that
counts.

Some county leagues are at a disadvantage
because the available waters in their area capable of
taking 120 or more anglers are limited – plus the
fact that these waters may hold mainly small fish

with a mere scattering of big fish, and the weights of catches seldom high. On such waters one man in a good swim could easily equal 50 other anglers' total catch. It could be one 3lb fish taken, and this would need a lot of minnows to equal it! This is a good case for employing the points system. Incidentally, it takes a lot of bank length to accommodate some 120 competitors with 15 yards between each.

All league teams are competing against each other, so providing a team-man can catch a few ounces in order to pick up several points he has achieved what he has set out to do. If each member in a team contributes a reasonable percentage of points, it will put the team in a fairly high position.

Most leagues are team events, and for the competing anglers a different approach is required than when fishing an individual open match. In a league event the team position is far more important and certainly more satisfying than individual positions; all anglers like to come top man of the day, but that should be secondary to getting a good team placing. A friendly rivalry between teams develops in a good league, and a close comradeship develops between team members.

Consistency is the hallmark of a good team angler, for he must take the maximum weight from his swim, however low that may be. He must catch something; even a few tiny fish can bring several valuable points.

A league competitor develops an all-round angling ability, for the different varieties of fish in different types of swims means that he must be able to fish in many ways and styles. Many top-class open circuit match-men are not suited to league fishing, for that type of angler is an individualist and always out to win. If he fails, the chances are he will have nothing to contribute to his team's score.

The attraction of league fishing is the companionship of teammates, the pooling of knowledge, discussions and pre-match planning. A week or two before a match, a team will get together to discuss such things as the venue, condition of the water, species to be caught, tackle, tactics, and the kind of bait best suited to luring the fish on to the hook.

Let him live to fight another day!

Care and quickness is needed when unhooking a fish during a contest. ALWAYS use a disgorger to unhook a fish unless it is very lightly lip-hooked. DON'T hurt a fish. It will provide sport on another day.

ANOTHER TOP TIP

Snap-on clips, two rubber stops, and a piece of brightly-painted aluminium make up this butt bite-indicator.

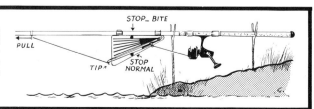

TEACH-IN
on river management

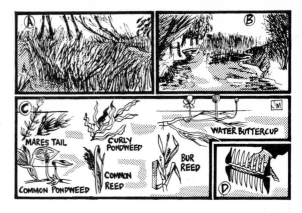

A RIVER that has become choked with weeds (Picture A) is useless for fishing. But it can be restored by careful 'thinning' (B). If all the weeds are ruthlessly destroyed there will be no food or shelter for the fish — so the weed-clearing should be underdone rather than overdone. The commonest and fastest-growing water weeds are illustrated in Picture C. Natural decomposition of the plants, if allowed to build up, will cause fermentation in the mud and silt to cause an extra demand on the available oxygen in the water – and fish die. A simple weed-clearing device can be made by tying together the heads of two garden rakes (D).

BREAM
Teach-in

AN average bream weighs 4lb. The fish (A) has a deep flat shape, rounded back and deeply-forked tail. The scales have a metallic lustre. Popular baits (B) are maggots, bread and lobworms. They are great feeders, so always have the landing net ready for action (C).

As the fish takes the bait (D), it lifts the weighted line which moves the float. Strike against the direction of the run of the fish (E), enabling the hook to secure itself in the stiff lips of the fighting bream.

TEACH-IN on casts

SOME fishermen walk for miles along a river bank. This is quite unnecessary, for by standing in one place (Picture A), every likely holding pool can be covered. When casting for game fish always make the first cast downstream and then work up. If the current is flowing too fast, the fly will drag and appear unnatural.

So practise putting a belly or a snake into the line as it falls on to the water (B). This allows the fly to travel without being dragged by the heavier line. Skilful anglers (central figure) are able to cast around hillocks and trees.

BY CASTING FROM ONE SPOT YOU CAN COVER A LARGE AREA OF RIVER

DIRECTION OF CURRENT

WINTER on the

by MICHAEL PRICHARD

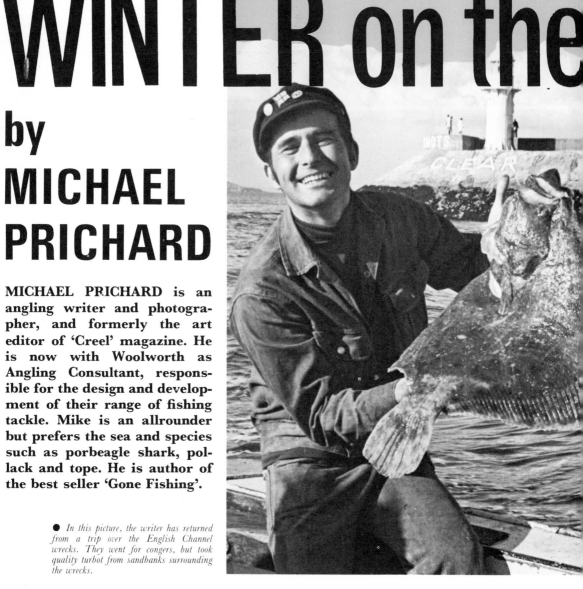

MICHAEL PRICHARD is an angling writer and photographer, and formerly the art editor of 'Creel' magazine. He is now with Woolworth as Angling Consultant, responsible for the design and development of their range of fishing tackle. Mike is an allrounder but prefers the sea and species such as porbeagle shark, pollack and tope. He is author of the best seller 'Gone Fishing'.

● *In this picture, the writer has returned from a trip over the English Channel wrecks. They went for congers, but took quality turbot from sandbanks surrounding the wrecks.*

THE icy wind, blowing flurries of snow from the Nor'-east, funnelled down from the mountains of Argyllshire on to the jumbled waters of the Firth of Clyde. Bouncing on the short waves, but held up the wind and tied by a slim anchor rope, rode a white, fibreglass dinghy. Three men, muffled against the bitter bite of the January blast, sat fishing.

This was the time of the big fish, Atlantic cod running in with swollen bellies to spawn in the sea loch of Scotland's west coast. The Firth is here, be-

tween the Cloch Lighthouse on the mainland and the small fairway light off the town of Dunoon. The Gantocks, as a sea angling mark, is made up of some underwater rocks, a gully through which the strong tide rips, and the wreck of a Swedish ore-carrying boat.

It sprang to prominence when three Edinburgh lads, 'The Trio', began to bring ashore huge catches of better-than-average fish. I went to Scotland to see what made this mark so productive and to share with Bill Freshwater, George Mann and Doug

GANTOCKS

Dinnie some of the fabulous cod fishing from the mark.

One can never be alone fishing the Gantocks, for it must be one of the busiest shipping lanes in the world. Huge tankers and atomic-powered submarines constantly ply back and forth, and it is just off the main channel that we anchored to avoid their wash. I'd asked about bringing bait for the fish, perhaps a couple of score of black Dungeness lugs? But, I was firmly told, the bait was taken care of and that all I would need was a general purpose boat rod, a stout reel filled with 30lb line and a few odd swivels.

Out in the boat, at anchor, I realised that we weren't using conventional hook baits at all. This was to be my introduction to the pirk! I had tried these artificial metal lures off the East Anglian coast for cod with little success, probably because in the polluted, mud-laden inshore waters no fish could see the lure working. And lures have to work, for they depend on the action built into them, either as a curve in a cast pirk or the bent shape of a metal tube filled with lead, to encourage cod to strike at them.

Basically what happens is this: The Trio try to anchor over the gully along which the migrating cod travel north to spawn. The wreck and rocks attract large numbers of small pollack and coalfish that live among the weed and underwater obstructions. Cod that have travelled in from the Atlantic are hungry when they arrive at the juction of the main channel that opens into a number of sea lochs. They feed on the small fish, and if anglers want to catch them they have to use a bait that simulates the action of a frightened or wounded fish.

The pirks, having an in-built weight, are lowered to the bottom then jigged up and down in a short, fluttering movement that excites heavy fish into striking at the lures. The lads have tried natural bait, mackerel, herring and worms but they aren't in the same class as the artificial. It is not fishing for the lazy angler – the bait has to be constantly on the move, fished sink and draw, occasionally raised up a fathom and then allowed to flutter down again to touch bottom.

We found that our arrival just after dead slack

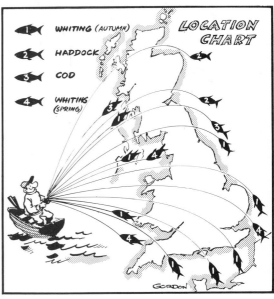

TEACH-IN...ON THE MOVEMENTS OF SEA FISH

SALTWATER fish follow broadly the same pattern of movement. To find a suitable spawning ground, the entire population may migrate across several miles of ocean.

In midsummer the small shoals of WHITING join together. By the autumn they are massed together for the spawning journey, which is believed to end near the Straits of Dover. By the spring, they are again in large shoals over the feeding grounds.

HADDOCK do not travel so far, but they have a similar seasonal movement. The best haddock fishing grounds are off the East coast of Scotland.

Cod are essentially cold water fish. They rarely shoal further South than The Wash and the coasts of East Anglia. But occasionally a small number will penetrate through the English Channel in winter.

SEEING IS BELIEVING!

The cameraman was on the spot to record this haul of huge cod from the Gantocks by 'The Trio' – George Mann, Doug Dinnie and Bill Freshwater. The six fish weighed over 140lb, the largest one being 38lb. They were all taken fishing a pirk in the gulley along which the large cod move inshore to spawn.

water gave us bites from smallish pollack, with the odd coalie putting in an appearance. These fish had ventured from the security of the wreck knowing that the far larger cod arrived with the flood tide, seeking food as they swam in from the deeper waters of the Firth.

Bill and Doug had both species, which they returned to the sea, then George got a pull from the first cod. It wasn't large and gave little trouble bringing it up to the boat.

With a strengthening tide flow, the pirks began to run out down beyond the stern. Bill says that the lures work better whenever the current begins to move; it stretches the line out, hanging the baits in the water a few inches off the sea bed. Then the lures really come into their own as the action imparted by raising and lowering the rod tip combines with the natural twisting imparted by the current.

The bites are solid, positive takes that almost wrench the rod from your hands. Fish seem to grab at the lure, no doubt, expecting it to dash away to cover. As the rod tip goes over in a tight arc the rod is lifted, meeting the power of the cod as it continues to swim uptide. Then the fun starts!

Bill had a fish that took the lure just as it hit the hard bottom. It came easily for a few feet, decided there was something wrong with the quickly-grabbed meal and dived for the gully. Bill's rod swung over hard with the tip meeting the waves. He held the fish, thumbs jammed on to the spool of his multiplier. There was no time to adjust the star drag, and anyway an angler's thumbs are far more sensitive in moments of crisis!

Gradually the combined power of rod and tide tired the fish and Bill began to get a few yards of nylon back on the reel. Steady pumping brought the cod, a fish of about 15lb up through the murk to lie quivering on the surface. Doug's gaff flashed and the fish came inboard. One cannot afford to make mistakes in landing fish from a tiny dinghy; there has to be team effort with only one man moving around in the boat. Small fish can be lifted on the pirk, but the bigger specimens need to be gaffed neatly and expertly.

Doug Dinnie was next to get a take. He had been working away with the rod, holding the butt steady while giving a sharp lift with the left arm, for a long time before anything had come to the lure. These big cod of winter do not appear to move in large shoals; they are more solitary in behaviour and you have to wait for them. By the same token, I do not believe that it is easy to find a suitable ground for these fish or to give hard and fast rules as to the phase of tide on which they will feed.

One has to be exact in placing the boat over a likely mark and then the bait must be worked continuously. Doug's efforts had been rewarded and he was into a heavy fish. It didn't run off with sharp, head-shaking movement but pulled ponderously against the compression of the rod. Doug had to

TEACH-IN on safety at sea

SEA ANGLING is the fastest-growing branch of our sport. But safety at sea is often neglected.

Charter boat skippers (Picture 1a) should make sure the boat is not overloaded and that lifejackets, flares and charts are carried. Rubber dinghies and rafts (Picture 1b) should be used only in sheltered bays and on inland waters. The

angler should still wear a lifejacket.

Keep a sharp eye on the clouds, which will give advance warning of a storm. And when the flag on the boat starts to blow (2), make for safety. A small pocket compass (3) is a useful aid to safety.

give line as it was stretched taut and singing. He thumbed lightly on the spool but still the nylon tore off in savage, sudden jerks.

This looked a good specimen and I wondered if Doug was once again playing the British record. He'd had the record cod, a fish from the Gantocks, but a few weeks before my visit he had seen his fish bettered by a local angler.

Both Bill and George had quietly reeled in their lures, sensing that Doug's was a huge fish and that he might need the help of his companions. As the fight progressed the jerking, diving pulls had gone and the cod began to lose the battle. It is at this stage that a big fish opens its mouth, gasping, and a further pressure against the angler comes into play – the power of the water! Then it is a hard haul against the flow of the tide, with the fish sometimes blowing up to the surface out beyond the stern.

This began to happen to Doug but he kept cool. As the cod showed, we knew that this was a monster as it gave the last despairing thrashes with its tail. Lying downtide, its weight kept Doug's rod wrenched round in a tight curve. He pumped steadily, unaware of the muttered advice given constantly by his pals.

It seemed ages before the fish came to the stern, but all the time it lay resting in the waves with fins fluttering as the nylon brought it closer to us. Bill busied himself with the short gaff, sank it below the surface and firmly drew it up into the solid shoulder of the cod. It took two hands, tightly grasped round the handle, to lift the fish into the boat where it lay flapping on the boards. A sharp tap with a priest and the fight was over.

The trio had a lot of good cod that day. The smaller ones were returned because these lads are careful to take only fish that they need. They are specimen hunters in the true sense, after the record but realising that there is little point in hammering the small fish that could be providing sport in the

Seeing is believing!

And you can still see it any time if you live near the Kent coast. This fine cod, weighing 50lb, was taken off Deal and it can still be seen, mounted in plastic in a cafe on the pier. How about that served up with a stone of chips!

TOP TIP

Don't bunch your bait

With this method the bait will not bunch at the bend of the hook. Tie a double overhand knot to a loop of line. Hooks are then easily changed. Pass the lot through the bait at Position A. The loop of the line is then opened and passed over the bait. Insert the hook from the underside at Position B.

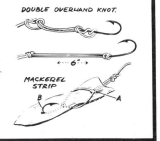

DOUBLE OVERHAND KNOT.

MACKEREL STRIP

future. These Edinburgh anglers are dedicated to their fishing; there is no element of luck in what they do or catch.

On this day there were other boats out from the clubs with men using the same lures, but nobody had the number or quality of fish that the Trio mustered. Their success is in their knowledge, gained over many fishing trips in all kinds of weather, the constant working of the lures and the awareness of the need to be continually adjusting their boat position relative to the state and power of the water that gushes into and out of the Clyde.

If and when the cod record is broken, my money would be on one of the 'Trio' to boat it from the Gantocks . . . probably during a snowstorm!

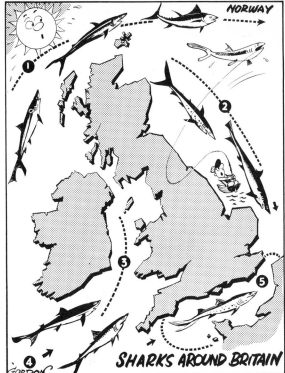

SHARKS AROUND BRITAIN

HOW TO CATCH THAT BIG 'UN !

ANGLERS after big quarry (A) are advised to bolt on the reel, and to use a tip-ring 'axle' that revolves. When the fish is hooked, a swivel-chair with a built-in rod butt rest is useful. Otherwise stomach and groin bruising could result.

The 'smell lane' is constantly charged (B) with morsels of blood, entrails and crushed fish offal. The mesh bag is trailed from the stern. Sometimes it is better to anchor the boat and let the ebb and flow of the tide carry the rubby-dubby.

The Thresher shark is not commonly caught on rod and line. All other species (C) frequent the Devon and Cornish coasts.

They like it HOT...

BIG-GAME fishing is no longer the sole pre-rogative of the Bahamas. It is a developing sport in Britain. But sharks will only stay where the water is warm.

During the summer, packs of the grey, sleek monsters move in at Area 4 from the Atlantic. The Gulf Stream takes them around the South coast of Ireland.

Blue-fin sharks and Tuna fish are particularly adventurous. They go on past the North coast of Scotland (Area 1) to the rich sea-fish feeding ground off Norway.

A few of the hunters come down the North Sea again (Area 2), where they damage the nets of commercial fishermen by slashing at the trawl to get at the fish.

Spurdogs and Tope – they always spend the winter season in the deeps of the English Channel (Area 5) – can be caught during warmer spells in Area 3.

But the Northern wanderings of these shark-like creatures never extends farther than The Wash or the Isle of Man.

and they like their fish FRESH

SHARK BAITING

ECHO SOUNDER

A

GORDON

B.

THE 'TIMETABLE' for catching shark revolves around the late summer months. Where the Gulf Stream meets the English Channel around Cornwall is a favourite feeding ground for the blue shark. They like warm water, and although the monsters range in the deep water, they do come near to the surface for food. The echo sounder is able to draw a picture of the sea-bed. It shows where the shark are likely to lie. On the way to the shark mark, which may be 10 or 12 miles offshore, fresh mackerel are caught. Anglers use them for bait (Picture A). The trace leading to the hook is made of alasticum wire. A large float (Picture B) is attached to the bait to control the depth at which it is fished.

TEACH-IN ... Survival in the Oceans

1.

2.

3.

GORDON

SEA PREDATORS

LIFE for all species of fish in the ocean is one long battle for survival. Because most fishes are carnivorous, the war is fierce. Speed, both for attack and defence, is brought to perfection in mackerel, shark and barracuda. Protective colourings and markings are a great help to the hunted.

The teeth of all sea-fish are backward pointing. This is for seizing the prey and not for tearing. The meal is usually swallowed whole. Picture 1 shows a codfish eating a mackerel.

Picture 2: A barracuda, which reaches a length of 8–10ft, hunts like the shark and devours fish as it goes. Picture 3: Herrings, pilchards and even larger fish such as salmon are consumed by the porpoise. The lovable mammal – often called a dolphin – is also a destroyer of lesser fish in large quantities.

LOOKING TO THE FUTURE

✳

DICK ORTON (pictured right), Organiser of The Angling Foundation, has long been connected with the sport. A twenty-five-year career in the tackle trade, first with Allcocks, then with the Shakespeare Co., concluded in 1972. Since then, his time has been devoted to writing, running the Foundation and fishing, his principal interest since boyhood. The pike is his favourite quarry, but everything else receives his periodic attention – from the lordly salmon to the humble eel.

DICK ORTON gives an insight to the quiet but important work being done by the Angling Foundation

GOD FORBID that we should ever suffer another roach-famine such as the one which struck us in the mid-sixties, but if we did we should be able to react far more quickly in replacing the lost fish because the necessary research is now well under way.

Rising costs of petrol and other essentials have forced the British people to look for leisure pursuits at somewhat lower cost than in recent years, and there is now a handbook in being to guide local authorities and others in the creation of low-cost fisheries located where people may reach them easily and cheaply. It is available free of charge to all who can make good use of it.

For these two advances, anglers have to thank the Angling Foundation, working with others in the one instance, alone in the other. The Angling Foundation is a body set up by the British fishing tackle industry through which it could reinvest a proportion of its earnings in the future welfare of the sport. Now it receives support also from tackle manufacturers outside this country for whom we are an important market.

When thoughts along these lines first germinated,

back in the late 1950s, dereliction, not over-exploitation, was then the immediate problem. Disused canals solid with weed; rotting lock-gates and collapsing weirs; bankside vegetation run riot along margins of lake, river and canal alike. Anglers often fished for a few shillings – even pence: little beyond token restocking – often to no practical purpose – was attempted by way of fishery management.

But by 1965, the tackle manufacturers and dealers of the day were aware that one of two things must clearly happen. Fisheries would continue to decline through pollution, water abstraction and neglect in detail; or public interest would at last be aroused in our water-spaces and public money spent.

It was seen that if public money were spent on a significant scale, there was little likelihood that the angler would be the sole beneficiary. And so, to some extent, it has been. The price of remedying things was an intense competition for the amenity, being boating in all its forms (often at very high density), skin-diving and water-skiing.

By 1970, the entire tackle trade, alarmed over the welfare of the sport, formed an off-shoot of the existing manufacturers' association and deliberated upon how it might best invest a levy from the trade. Money, so the trade felt, was not all it had to offer. By making and selling fishing tackle one does not necessarily become an expert captor of specimen fish or handsome trophies; but in dealing with such people, directly and indirectly, an insight into the realities of the sport is acquired on a scale open to few others.

The inaugural meeting of the Foundation took place in December 1970. A Council was elected and policy guide-lines laid down. John Goddard, equally well known as a tackle maker and angling publicist, was the first chairman – appropriately enough, for he was among the first to see the need for a new initiative from the trade. Rapidly, money rolled in. Strange to relate, requests for help from

suitable applicants did not keep pace. By the end of 1972 a modestly substantial fund had accumulated, but not much money had been disbursed. Many and varied were the projects which had been debated.

Real achievements at that stage included donations to charitable undertakings, such as Douglas Bader's, to help with fishing for the disabled; the provision of sets of coloured wall-charts to assist the newly-qualified angling instructors then appearing on the scene; the offer of a scholarship to the newly-formed Institute of Fisheries Management. Also, money was given to the organisation which fought successfully to defend Snowdonia (the source of many important gamefish rivers) against the threat of opencast mining for copper and other metal ores. Founding grants to set up Anglers' Consultatives were made. But still a large lump of indigestible money stuck in the pipe-line.

The turning-point came in 1973, early in the year when £2,440, the largest sum to that date voted, was promised to Dr Anne Powell of the Biology Department of the Sir John Cass School of Science and Technology to expand and sustain research already started into the breeding biology of roach.

This fitted the Foundation's terms of reference to perfection. While money may be given for purely charitable purposes, this is not 'mainstream'. The Foundation exists, so to speak, to identify squeaks in the machinery where a penn'orth of oil *NOW* will save a pound's worth of reconstruction later on. The wisdom serves to detect the squeak; the cash figures as the 'oil'. It is the capacity to deploy both without fear or favour over a broad front which gives the Foundation its unique type of usefulness to anglers in Britain.

Soon after the grant for roach-research the Foundation announced its biggest venture to date – a gold medal award scheme to honour those in industry who have made conspicuous contribution

TOP TIP on Bite Indicators

Fishing at night is on the increase and the use of bite-indicators is flourishing. Some anglers find that the clothes peg type of fitting interferes with casting and tangles the line. But if you solder the bell to a short length of curtain spring wire and then insert half a bicycle spoke, solder it at the other end of the spring, and screw the assembly into the swing tip eye at the end of the fishing rod, the faults are corrected. If the rod-tip fitting is of the push-in type, substitute the bicycle spoke for a nail inserted in the core of a ballpoint pen refill.

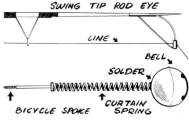

to the restraint or avoidance of pollution and to the conservation of water. Within a month, many applications for entry forms came from firms large and small.

Activity continues in other fields – publications; a grant to coordinate the coaching of angling; another to help produce instructional films; help for the organisation of competitive fly-fishing in Britain. But where next? That is largely a question of wider support and fresh funds.

Regretfully, not all tackle firms give their support. As matters stand, the Foundation has now bit- ten off pretty well as much as it is able to chew. It is not open to public membership as such, but any who derive their livelihood in whole or in part from the sport of angling are eligible for one of the categories of membership.

The Foundation does not think the time has yet come for trumpet-blowing, but a modest pride is taken in what has been achieved with an income of around £8,000 per annum, less than 20 per cent of which finances its total administration.

WINTER BY THE RIVERSIDE

WINTER on the Thames and this angler is certainly dressed for the part. There is nothing worse than being cold when you are fishing, so do dress with warm clothing. One tip is to wear your pyjamas under your fishing outfit – especially if you plan to fish all day in the same swim, as with match-fishing.

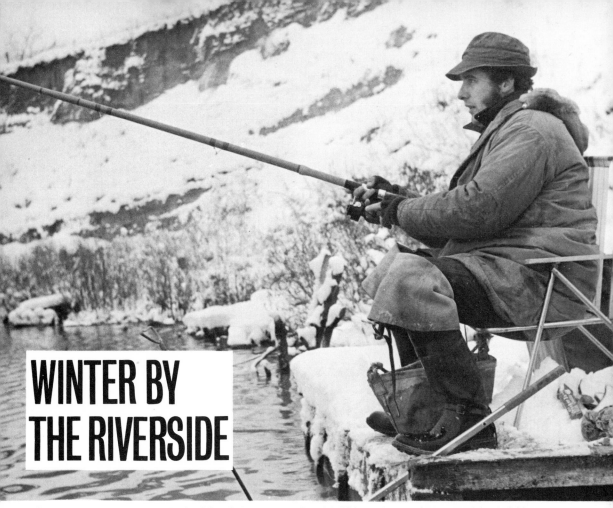

WINTER BY THE RIVERSIDE

SNOW on the banks and too cold for fishing? Don't you believe it! This angler caught very good roach fishing maggot bait on float tactics. But it is important to keep the bait warm until it is put on the hook. Use a small tin to hold the maggots and keep it in an inside pocket of your jacket.

TOP TIP for dishwashers...

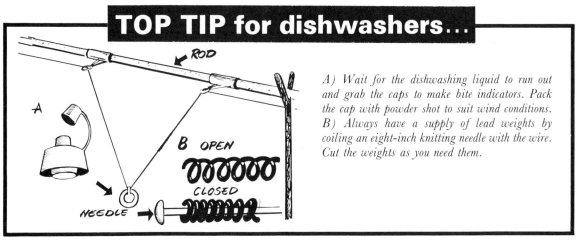

A) Wait for the dishwashing liquid to run out and grab the caps to make bite indicators. Pack the cap with powder shot to suit wind conditions.
B) Always have a supply of lead weights by coiling an eight-inch knitting needle with the wire. Cut the weights as you need them.

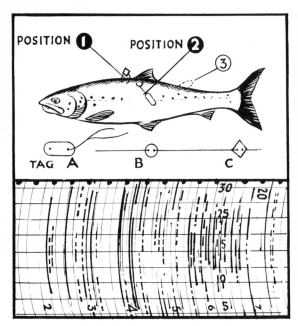

TEACH~IN on counting fish

IN the top left picture, we see the method used by the Ministry of Ag and Fish to keep tabs on the movements, the feeding grounds and growth rates of salmon. The small fish (smolts) are checked and tagged just before they enter the sea on the downward migration from the river.

Tags B and C are made of grey or clear plastic and fastened with silver wire at Position 1. Tag A is of green plastic and fastened with nylon thread at Position 2. The adipose fin at 3 is of no use to the fish and sometimes it is clipped off so that particular fish can be identified again.

Several methods of labelling fish are constantly exper-

imented with. But no method can be 100 per cent satisfactory, as the tags rub off.

On the right, our artist has given a diagram of how the fish are counted on the upward migration. The fish are guided by a funnel-shaped aperture through a tube, where they pass an electronic recorder where they are shown on a graph.

In the graph (bottom left) it will be seen that leaves, twigs and even grass are capable of making fluttering marks. The only true record can be observed on film, and the experts are working on that now.

TOP TIP for the beach and pier anglers

Boat fishermen use a 'rubby dubby' mesh bag of liver, blood, entrails and mashed fish to attract shark. The stationary beach and pier angler has always wanted to copy the method. This is how it can be done. Saturate the sponge in pilchard oil and wire it to the top of the lead sinker. Fish cannot resist the globules which lead them to the baited hook.

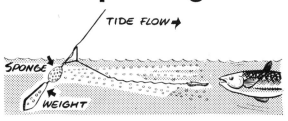

Conrad Voss Bark

❝The new lures have splendid names which attract anglers as well as fish...❞

FLY FISHING for LAKE TROUT

CONRAD VOSS BARK is a writer and journalist and author of 'Fishing For Lake Trout', which urged fishermen to adopt more skilful and delicate methods of fly-fishing on lakes – instead of using large, multi-coloured lures. He is a contributor to several angling magazines and first fished Blagdon in the 1930's. Known nationally for many years for his reports on Parliament in the BBC's radio and television news.

FLY FISHING for lake trout opens up a whole new world of opportunity for anglers. It is still a comparatively new sport and is still developing. But already it is providing some of the best fishing in England. And new lake fisheries are now being opened every year. In the last 30 years more than 250 fisheries have been opened and stocked, mostly with big rainbow trout.

Many of these fisheries issue day tickets at between £2–£5 a day. Other fisheries are on a subscription basis. Subscriptions for a year cost from £100–£150 for one day's fishing a week. For this you can catch up to four or five rainbow trout in a day – if you're lucky or skilful enough – and they are really big fish.

At one of the most famous lake fisheries in Hampshire, Two Lakes, the average trout caught weighs nearly 2½lb and each year many trout of 5lb or over are taken. One or two weigh over 10lb. These fish are the size of salmon, they fight well, and taste good. Each year, too, they seem to grow bigger – the result of good management policy and the rich feed provided in these shallow, plankton-full lakes.

Lake fishing is not only confined to commercial fisheries designed expressly for that purpose. Several hundred reservoirs up and down the country provide good fly fishing for both brown and rainbow trout, and these are big fish too, particularly at reservoirs like Blagdon, Chew and Grafham. At reservoirs you are merely likely to catch fewer fish, on average, because of the bigger expanse of water and because, again on average, reservoirs are not so heavily stocked.

The main difference between lake and river fishing is simply the difference between still and moving water. On a river, the current takes your fly and drifts it down to the fish or swirls it around downstream. It is the movement that attracts the fish. On lakes, where there is little or no moving water, it is the angler and not the current that has to give the movement to the fly.

The traditional way of lake fishing was developed from techniques used in fishing for sea trout on Scottish lochs. One fly, or sometimes several, is tied on your nylon leader, and cast out either from a drifting boat or from the bank. The fly is allowed to sink a little way and then retrieved by the angler pulling in line with one hand while he holds the rod with the other.

This is lure fishing, sometimes called wet-fly fishing, and is still very popular on lakes and reservoirs though the original methods have been enormously expanded in the last 20 years. It is now possible, thanks to the development of plastics, nylon, and fibre glass, to cast the lure or fly much greater distances with lighter rods, making it easier to fish all day without fatigue.

The Americans developed the shooting head – a short, heavy length of plastic line spliced to monofilament. The plastic line – the shooting head – with the nylon leader and lure on the end is worked into the air by the rod, backwards and forwards, until sufficient momentum is developed. Then it is released and shoots forward carrying the thin monofilament backing with it. By using the shooting head with an ordinary 9ft trout rod, the lure can be cast 30 and sometimes 40 yards. Anglers fishing from the bank can cover twice the amount of water with a shooting head than is possible with an ordinary double-taper line.

Plastic lines can be constructed with a lighter density than water, in which case they are virtually unsinkable. Others, of a heavier density, sink at a controlled rate. Some lines now have lead cores so that they can sink right to the bottom at a high speed. All these developments have made it possible to fish the fly at any depth the angler wants, and on the large reservoirs big rainbows are sometimes taken on the bottom 40 or 50 feet down. Sophisticated equipment of this kind means that the angler can now reach the trout wherever they are.

Then there are the 'flies' which are really lures, of which there are now thousands of patterns. The original Scottish-type wet flies such as the Peter Ross, the Butcher, and Mallard and Claret, were at least flies in the sense that though they looked like no fly that ever existed they had sloped-back feather 'wings' and bodies of fur or tinsel. But the new lures

Teach-In on fly fishing

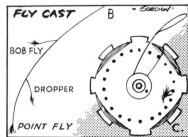

68

A rainbow trout of 13½lb – above the British record fish – is put into a Kent lake by the head bailiff Peter Leith. Such fish are raised on fish farms in the country by feeding them with pellet food. The water is Sundridge Lake, near Sevenoaks, and a season ticket costs well above £100.

MONSTER!

THERE was a time when it was the done thing to place a fly-reel about 15 inches along the butt. Now the reel is right at the end of the rod. To control the drop of the fly when wielding the rod, the correct grip is illustrated in Picture A. Notice the thumb extended and pointing forward. Loose line is peeled off between each false cast. When retrieving or guiding the fly through the currents, the line is held as shown in bottom right of Picture A.

Cast carriers (Picture B) enable the angler to see what combination of flies are ready for use. Made of plastic, the disc has a revolving centre piece, which when gripped between thumb and forefinger allows the nylon leader to be rolled off after the leader (cast) has been looped over the line. And when packing-up, the leader and the flies are coiled back on to the disc before detaching the assembly from the line.

Many anglers just use a point fly, or one point fly and a dropper. A third fly, which is called the bob fly, dances along the top of the water and it will often take a fish when the line is being retrieved.

developed in recent years, again mainly in America, are made of all kinds of materials from plastics to clipped deer hair, with long streamer bodies sometimes of whole feathers. They have splendid names – the Muddler Minnow, Rusty Rat and Old Nic – which attract anglers as well as fish.

The fact is that lake trout can be caught on almost any kind of lure that stimulates them to take it in their mouths – they take a lure, it is believed, mainly from curiosity – and anglers have made use of this knowledge for many years. My grandfather, old Willie Cox of Bristol, caught many good trout in the newly-opened Blagdon reservoir from 1904–1913 on large salmon flies which he cast with a double-handed, 16ft greenheart salmon rod.

So you see that although we have new materials

Teach-In on fly fishing

COARSE fishermen are stealing the thunder from expert trout fishermen by beating them at their own game of catching fish on delicate tackle. All coarse fish will take creepers, flies and nymphs if presented to them correctly and at the right depth. But the most consistent risers to a fly in the coarse fish world are dace, bleak, perch, rudd, roach and chub.

On hot summer days, the fish are lying on the bottom so select a fly (Picture A in diagram below) which fishes deep and which resembles a small fish or grub. Cover the water systematically as in Picture B and always start by casting upstream.

Take advantage of concealment. If the river bank has no covering shrubbery, approach the fishing spot from a crouching position as in Picture C1. If there are trees try to get underneath them so that your silhouette merges with the trees and casts no shadows to scare the fish.

A.

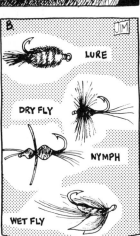

LURE

DRY FLY

NYMPH

WET FLY

RIGHT   C.

WRONG

A
SELECTING YOUR FLY

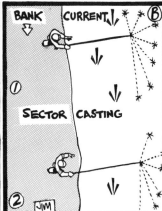

BANK   CURRENT
1
SECTOR CASTING
2   JIM

C2

FLY FISHING, which is the gentlest of all the angling arts, is never hurried or erratic. It was once practised only by the well-bred and the high-born. But today every angler wants to be able to cast a fly. A balanced outfit of rod, reel and line will cost anything from £15 to £50.

When fishing, the angler must always try to keep out of sight of the fish by blending into the surroundings as in Picture A in the diagram on the left. In Picture B, we see what the different kinds of flies look like. The lure resembles beetles, grubs, shrimps or small fish. Dry flies are fished on the surface and must be dressed with hackles that repel moisture. Nymphs depict the underwater stage of insect life and are the tastiest of morsels. Fish go mad on them. Wet flies resemble the sunken insect.

The correct angle for a fly to work in the water (Picture C) is when the artificial dressing is at right angles to the bend of the hook. To achieve this, pull the nylon knot very tight.

he had never heard of, and many different types of lures he could never have imagined, the essential basic method of fishing a lure does not and cannot change very much. We can cast more easily now, with lighter rods, and everything we use is more sophisticated but the basic principle is just the same. The lure is cast out as far as possible and retrieved at varying depths and varying speeds until a fish takes. Then there is a bang on the rod, the rod top bends, the reel sings, and the fish is on.

Lure fishing has several disadvantages, the obvious one being that it can become monotonous. If you go to the big reservoirs like Chew or Grafham on the opening day of the season you can see several hundred anglers all standing thigh deep in water, crowded along the banks, casting and casting without pause for hour after hour with an almost hypnotic regularity. Another disadvantage is that it is in some ways unintelligent fishing. It is similar in its basic approach to spinning. You cover as much water as possible and hope that a fish will be stimulated or provoked to take.

Fortunately, lure fishing is by no means the only method of catching lake trout, and not always is it the most effective.

Round about the time that Willie Cox was catching trout at Blagdon on salmon flies, another angler on the same water, Dr Bell of Wrington, began to open up the stomachs of the trout that were caught in order to examine what they had been feeding on. He extracted large numbers of quite small insects, midge pupae and larvae, nymphs, and water beetles or corixae. If these were what the trout lived on, why should they not take flies, very small flies, dressed to look like these insects and fished in the same way the insects themselves moved, instead of lures, which represented no natural food insects at all?

So Dr Bell constructed a whole series of patterns dressed to represent these insects – Blagdon Buzzer, which was an imitation of a midge pupa, the Amber Nymph, and about a dozen other nymph-like patterns which represented actual trout food. Instead of being cast out and stripped in fast, they were allowed to drift or else twitched in very slowly with delicate movements through the water to imitate the actual movement of insects.

At first, all the lure anglers laughed at Dr Bell's little flies with their natural dull brown and olive colourings. But they did not laugh for long. Dr Bell began to catch fish, far more than he had caught before with lures or wet flies. By the late 1920s old

Willie Cox and many other Blagdon anglers, following Dr Bell's example, had switched over to nymph fishing. Once they had done so they never went back to lure fishing, except occasionally. Nymph fishing had become much more fascinating.

Now it has developed enormously. Many books have been written about it. Fishing the nymph catches the imagination. It is a skilful method, not easily mastered, and has its own particular excitements.

The technique is, in theory, simple enough. The nymph pattern is an imitation or suggestion of one of the trout's natural food forms – the nymph of the lake olive or the pupa of the sedge fly and the midge. These pupae or nymphs rise from the bed of the lake to the surface of the water where they hatch into the adult fly. Trout take them avidly at all depths and especially when they rise in their thousands to the surface to hatch. Midge pupae in

Tempting the fish

SOMETIMES fish are just out of reach or they have to be tempted to feed. Expert coarse fishermen use a throwing stick (1), made from a hollow tube fitted to a stick or to the butt-piece of an old rod. They sometimes knead the bait into a ball of moistened bread or clay and shoot it by catapult (2).

When the fish start feeding, they are brought nearer with a bait dropper which can be made from a plastic hair curler (3). The maggots in the curler gradually escape. To catch a trout under inaccessible bushes, a bubble float (4) can be used to float flies down.

PLACING THE BAIT WHERE THE FISH ARE...
① THROWING STICK — END FILLED WITH MAGGOTS OR OTHER GROUND BAIT
②a CATAPULT ②b 'KNEADING' GROUND BAIT
③ BAIT DROPPER — WEIGHTED HAIR CURLER
④ FLY — BUBBLE FLOAT

particular hang just below the surface film in vast
numbers while waiting to hatch.

The angler watches for a hatch to take place and
fishes the appropriate pattern near or just under the
surface near the place where the trout are seen rising. If no hatch is taking place he fishes his nymph
pattern near the places where nymphs are likely to
be – in or near weed beds – or else goes searching for
a trout he can see and casts the nymph gently in
front of the fish.

Unlike a lure fisherman, a nymph fisherman does
not need to make long casts. He has to keep himself
well concealed. He fishes quietly and moves the fly
gently without disturbing the water. Mostly he does
not need to wade, and if he does wade he has to be
very careful not to disturb the water. A fish that has
been disturbed by movement, splashes, line wake,
thumping, noise of any kind, is a fish that is not
likely to take natural food until it recovers. The
nymph fisherman has to deceive the trout into
thinking it is taking its natural food.

This was a revolutionary new way of fishing. It
was as delicate and skilful a method as that of the
chalk streams, hitherto regarded as the highest pin-
nacle of the art of the fly, and just as intellectually
fascinating and absorbing. Many angling writers
rushed into print with new methods, new patterns,
new techniques – T. C. Ivens, C. F. Walker, Frank
Sawyer, Richard Walker and John Goddard.

The angler's equipment is fairly simple. The
nymph fisherman rarely uses a shooting head or
sinking plastic lines. Mostly he will have a split cane
or light fibreglass rod of about 8ft 6in with a very
light, double-tapered floating line. His nylon leader
will be long – never less than 12ft and often as long
as 14ft. This will be greased to within a foot or so of
the end, if he is fishing on the surface, or ungreased
if he wants his leader to sink.

If he is fishing deep, he will use a nymph pattern
which has had lead or copper wire wound under the
dressing to make it sink, and a really long leader of
up to 20ft. He conceals himself as well as he can on
the bank and casts out to where he can see the fish
or where he expects them to be and allows the
nymph to sink. It will take a long while.

As it sinks, he watches the nylon leader at the
point where it enters the water. At the slightest sign
of movement, a mere flicker of the nylon, he tight-
ens at once. When the nylon has sunk completely
he watches the end of his line. The line acts as a
float. Only then does he begin a very slow and
gentle retrieve, trying to imitate the movement of an

One man and his dog...

See the little dog in our picture? Gordon Smith, of Tunbridge Wells, Kent, says that if his dog couldn't go on his weekly fishing trip he'd be very unhappy. Says Gordon: 'He loves to watch me fishing and when I land a trout.' Or in this case, boat a trout.

insect rising slowly to the surface. If the trout takes it does so quietly. There is no bang on the rod top – only a slight movement of the line. The angler has to tighten at once or the fish will be missed. It will have felt the hardness of the fly and ejected it.

Tremendous concentration is needed in nymph fishing if the takes are to be seen and fish hooked. I once went fishing with an angler who had five takes in quick succession and missed them all. Even when he saw the take he was too late on the strike and two of them were so gentle he did not realise a trout was on. When I shouted 'strike' it was too late. The fly had been thrown.

One of the new generation of nymph fishermen is Brian Clarke, author of *The Pursuit of Stillwater*

Trout. We were once walking along the edge of a lake at Avington chattering away together, but his eyes were searching the water and suddenly he said: 'There's a fish!' While I was still looking he had unshipped his rod, unhooked his fly from the ring, and cast towards a weed bed only a few yards from the bank. On the second cast he tightened and was in to a rainbow of well over 2lb.

I was full of admiration. That was a brilliant demonstration of how to locate, cast to, and take a fish. I had never even seen that trout lurking in the weed. But he had. And that is the art of the nymph. Once you are hooked on this method you will never go back to the lure. It is the most exciting fishing you can imagine.

TEACH-IN on water plants

QUITE wrongly, coarse fish anglers violently hate water plants. They seek to destroy the 'weeds' to make a clear space to fish.

A fish will only hang around where it feels safe. The wholesale removal of weeds not only destroys all protective cover, but it also takes away the tiny organisms that make up a fish's diet.

Plants which should be kept under control but not destroyed are: 1) Common Reeds, grows in the margins. 2)

Water Buttercup, found on the shallows. 3) Starwort, acts as a water filter. 4) Canadian Pondweed, also a filter of silted water. 5) Dense Pondweed, densest on shallow water. 6) Curly Pondweed, prefers slow moving water. 7) Mare's Tail, suitable to settled water, where insect life gathers in profusion at the roots.

Willow trees grow very fast, and they should be cut alternately, as in top left.

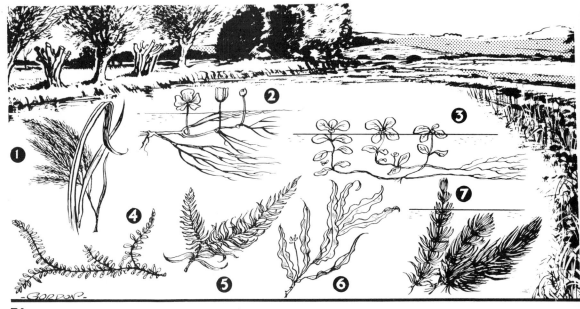

SIX

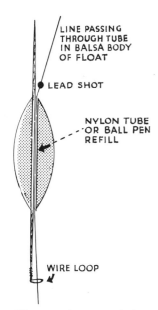

LINE PASSING THROUGH TUBE IN BALSA BODY OF FLOAT

LEAD SHOT

NYLON TUBE OR BALL PEN REFILL

WIRE LOOP

● Floats, wherever they are positioned in the water, cause drag on the line. To reduce water resistance when a fish takes the bait, use the idea shown here.

WITHDRAW

9"

V CUT

FLAT WOOD

● After a day's fishing, the waders often stick to swollen feet and it is a task for two people to get the boots off. The tip shown here makes it all so easy.

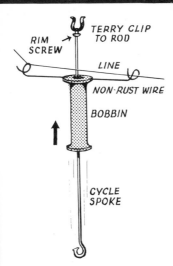

RIM SCREW

TERRY CLIP TO ROD

LINE

NON-RUST WIRE

BOBBIN

CYCLE SPOKE

● *The slightest movement of the bait by an inquisitive fish will straighten the line and send the bobbin flying pell-mell up the spoke.*

TOP

● *To make a spoon spinning lure that works like a charm, cut off the handle, punch two holes then add a swivel split ring and treble hook.*

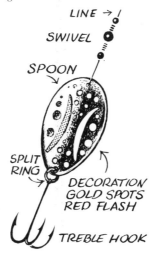

LINE →

SWIVEL

SPOON

SPLIT RING

DECORATION GOLD SPOTS RED FLASH

TREBLE HOOK

1) Anti-kink leads of various sizes — A, B, C in diagram below — are easily and quickly changed by using a brass safety pin (D), which is whipped to the line.

2) Carrots can tempt pike. Make them into plug baits as shown.

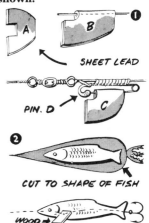

SHEET LEAD

PIN. D

CUT TO SHAPE OF FISH

WOOD

● Waders and wellingtons take a long time to dry out if they are not stored properly. A stuffing of old newspapers also helps.

TIPS

MAKE A ROD

'*Work slowly and with care and i*

CHARLES WADE is never happier than when he is among his friends and countrymen in the North-East. Here he is (right) with a good-looking Rays Bream after a day out on the Northumbrian coast.

OF YOUR OWN

will be as good as any you can buy— and several pounds less expensive'

by CHARLES WADE

FOR general fishing from beaches, piers and rocks, a rod of straight-tapered hollow glass, 11ft long and to cast weights of 3–5oz, cannot be bettered. It will do for bass, flatfish, rays and conger in the summer, and cod and whiting in the winter.

A one-piece rod is the best of all, being without the weakness of a joint and simple to make.

Buy the glass blank from a reputable tackle dealer and purchase seven intermediate rings and a lined tip ring that fits tightly over the tip of your rod. Do not be tempted to buy cheap rings.

If you use one of the popular multiplier reels you do not need any reel fitting on the rod. Just slip a length of rubber or plastic tube down the rod (about a foot of it) so that when you use the screw-on clamps supplied with the reel, it comes in the middle of the tubing at a point 25–30in from the extreme butt end of the rod. Glue the tubing in position. Another six-inch length fitted to the butt end makes the lower hand grip and you can glue on a rubber slipproof end as on a walking stick to finish off, or carve a mushroom-shaped hardwood knob, gluing the 'stem' part up inside the hollow end of the rod butt.

Now whip on the rings, the first one about 27in above the reel, the rest spaced in line at something like the following measurements: 17, $14\frac{1}{2}$, 12, 10, $9\frac{1}{2}$ and $6\frac{1}{2}$in. Then fit the tip ring.

Before whipping on the rings with terylene or nylon thread, file down the ends of each ring strut where they lie on the rod so that the whipping does not go over a bump. Start each whipping by laying the end of the thread on the rod about $\frac{1}{8}$in from the ring strut (you put sticky tape round the other strut to keep it in position while you whip down the first

one) and, with the reel of thread in the free hand, revolve the rod away from yourself, laying the turns over the loose end. Cut off the end when six turns have been made and continue whipping tightly up the slope of the strut.

When only six turns remain to be made, make a loop in 1ft of thread and lay it on the rod and complete the whipping turns towards the closed end of the loop. Cut off the thread, leaving a couple of inches, push the end through the loop and pull firmly on the other end of the loop to bring the tag end of the whipping thread under the last six turns and out. Trim the end close with a new razor blade.

Having completed the rest of the whippings, rub a little yacht varnish into each whipping, smoothing it in with a forefinger. A small brush is used to varnish under the ring where your finger won't go. When all is dry, varnish the whole rod, again using the forefinger dipped in varnish, doing the spaces between each ring in one operation. Use smooth, long strokes to lay on the varnish without bubbles or runs.

The rod is now finished and will have saved you several pounds on the price of a shop-bought rod.

Fixed-spool reels do not have rod clamps on them, so if you use one you will first have to fit a screw reel fitting on the rod. Buy it when you get the blank and test it for size in the shop, sliding it down from the tip of the blank until it lodges firmly where it must go, fixed reel clip towards the butt. Glue it in place with epoxy-resin adhesive after first sliding on any rubber or plastic tube handgrips you require. Make sure the rings are whipped on in line with the fixed reel clip.

If you use public transport to get to your fishing spots you must have a two-piece rod. You must either saw the blank in half carefully with a fine junior hacksaw and fit reinforced chromed-brass ferrules with epoxy-resin, or buy a two-piece blank that has ferrules or a spigot joint already fitted. Some shops supply blanks in this form.

A spigot joint is a piece of glass, glued into the end of the butt section, which is tapered and fits up inside the hollow end of the top section. Make sure you make a tight whipping for about an inch, starting about $\frac{1}{4}$in from the end of the top section. This prevents the blank splitting when in use – and a similar one where the spigot emerges from the butt section.

As the sea rod just outlined makes a versatile tool for general shore fishing, not being either an ultra-light bass rod or a very powerful heavy-duty rod, but a compromise, so an easy-actioned two-piece

tubular glass rod of the same length of 11ft makes the best all-round, freshwater coarse-fishing rod. It will be neither stiff, with only the tip flexible (such as a match-fishing rod), nor floppy. It will be suitable for most types of coarse fishing, from catching dace and roach to battling it out with barbel, big chub, tench and carp up to around 10lb or so, with lines of 3–7lb.

Ask for an Avon-type blank at the tackle shop. It is possible to buy ready-ferruled or spigot-jointed blanks of 11ft although there are more 10ft sets available. These will do at a pinch if you cannot get the longer set.

If the blank is not ferruled, buy a set of bronzed brass lightly-reinforced ferrules and fit them on with epoxy-resin adhesive. Just make sure you do not push the female ferrule too far on to the butt joint, or the whole length of the other ferrule will not go into it.

But before doing any ferrule fitting you have to make a cork handle. Buy enough cork rings from the shop to make a 26in handle. You simply push them on to the thin end of the butt section, leaving an inch of glass bare at the butt end, gluing them to the rod and to each other as you go. Keep four corks in

LIFE ALONG THE SEASHORE

AT VERY low spring tides, vast areas of seashore are exposed. It is then that 'razors' – an excellent bait for most sea fish – are revealed. They have an urge to bore deep, so that rocks are not the best place to look for razor fish. It is more profitable to explore the clear sandy patches between the rock outcrops.

Walk backwards (A) over the wet sand, and when a blow-hole shows up, stick the spear (B) into the mouth of the hole where the shell aperture can be felt. Twist, and pull evenly. Clumsy work with the spear will leave the juicy white foot of the razor fish anchored in the sand. The remainder is useless for bait.

The complete shell of the razor can be seen (C) before the flesh (D) has been taken out. Before the tide returns, it can be advantageous to poke the spear into rock crevices (E), where a lobster or crab may take hold.

reserve – they are normally $\frac{1}{2}$–$\frac{5}{8}$in wide – to allow for finishing the ends of the handle later on.

When the glue has set hard, use medium-grade glasspaper tacked to a six-inch piece of board and rub down the corks, working lengthwise on a table. Keep turning the handle to keep the finished job nicely rounded. Ordinary sliding reel fittings will be used and they are best bought with an inside diameter of about $\frac{13}{16}$in, to slide over a finished parallel cork handle.

When you still have to remove $\frac{1}{8}$in of cork to be able to slide on the reel fittings – keep testing as you work by holding a reel fitting to the cork – swap over to very fine glasspaper. Failure to do this early enough in the shaping is the cause of rough cork handles produced by many amateur rod builders. When the reel fittings will just not go over the corks, change the abrasive paper yet again to a very fine grade of silicon carbide, like that used for rubbing down the paintwork on car bodies. This ensures a really smooth handle.

Now stick on the remaining corks at each end of the handle, after putting the reel fittings on. When the glue has dried hard, sand the end corks down to a scroll shape, leaving them wider than the parallel handle between to prevent the reel fittings sliding right off. Also plug the open end of the butt with a suitable cork glued in.

You need eight chromed intermediate rings and matching tip and butt rings lined with pink

RESTOCKING is a very important part of fishery management. A speedy transfer of fish from the rearing farm to the new abode is essential for a 100 per cent survival rate.

Road transport is better than rail, because (as in Picture A), delivery is made right to the waterside.

Picture B shows the bailiffs examining fish for signs of disease. The bath, which has a perforated panel, is lowered into the water, avoiding sudden changes in temperature as the new arrivals swim out in their own time.

TEACH-IN
on
restocking

Picture C: A few fish dropped about every 20 yards is better than 200 in the same spot.

Approaching spawning time, ripe fish are 'impounded' and stripped of the eggs by a gentle massage (D). A stripping-block holds the fish steady as the eggs are milked into a bucket.

ceramic. Whip them on in the same way as for the sea rod, but use a very fine thread. The butt ring should be about 16in above the top of the cork handle and there should be two rings (one butt ring and one intermediate ring) on the handle section. Fit the rest on the top section, decreasing the spaces between them until the next-to-tip ring is about 6in from the extreme tip.

If the rod is spigot-joined, whip for $\frac{1}{2}$in in the same places as advised for the sea rod. If the rod has metal ferrules, whip for $\frac{1}{4}$in where they join the glass, just to finish off neatly.

Varnish as for the sea rod, but add a second coat when the first overall coat has dried hard – after about a week first rubbing the varnish down gently with silicon-carbide paper, very fine, used wet. This provides a key for the final coat. Wipe the rod down with a damp 'leather' to clean off specks of dirt before the final coat, which must be applied to a dry surface.

That's all there is to it. Work slowly and with care and the rod you make will be as good as any you can buy in the shops, and will be several pounds less expensive.

It is always an added pleasure to catch fish on a rod of one's own making.

They're taking a strong line...

Too much surface weed in the lake usually means slightly stronger tackle – which is what these three youngsters in a free water at Keston in Kent had to chat about. The lake contains massive carp, · and lines of about 12lb really are needed to beat the water lilies.

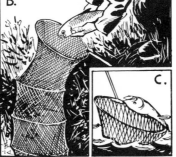

TEACH-IN ...here's how to handle a fish

BECAUSE a fish is a cold-blooded creature it does not sense pain as we know it. But great harm can be done to a fish by handling it. The human hand, unless wet, will scald the fish and burn off the coating of protective slime around the scales. The fish is then less resistant to disease. Taking care of the fish means:

- *PICTURE A: Keep the line tight and the grip firm when using a disgorger – or the line should be cut off close to the hook. (A metal hook is soon dissolved in intestinal juices, but a length of nylon will pass through the vent and trail with the fish.)*
- *PICTURE B: Use a wide net and keep the spacing rings open.*
- *PICTURE C: This fish is clumsily netted. Always pass the mouth of the net under the fish and low in the water before attempting to lift it.*

Don't be wet!

FISHING is not so funny if you fall in or get wet. And wearing a deerstalker hat (Picture A) is not foolish or feudal – it has a peak fore and aft to keep the sun out of your eyes and the raindrops from dripping down your neck.

When wading, the water is 'dammed back' to build up around the tops of the thigh-boots, and unthinking anglers often find the water trickling down to their feet. And when standing for a long time in the same spot, the weight of the angler causes him to sink gradually into the mud. So when moving to another place, always ease the boots out singly to prevent a stumble backwards.

To keep the trajectory of the hooks and weights clear of the head when casting (Picture B), never drop the rod tip below the one o'clock position.

And regularly check the condition of the studs/cleats on rubber waders. Smooth soles cannot give a grip, and they spell danger.

THE CANA

ALF WALKER (above) now lives in Ontario and has been in the tackle and gun trade all his life. He was born in Northumberland and was twice winner of the North of England casting title. He is an acknowledged authority on the haul technique of single-hand distance fly casting, and a noted European tournament caster. He was also an angling instructor for the Scottish Tourist Board and casting tutor for the Scottish Recreation Council.

DIAN SCENE

Photograph by Elliott G. Deighton

This land of vast distances with the finest assortment of fishing in the world...

by Alf WALKER

CANADA offers a wide range of fishing, contained within a vast 4,000-mile territory from Newfoundland to Vancouver Island, bordered by the Atlantic on the east, the Arctic to the north and the Pacific on the west. The land is latticed by rivers and streams and contains a mosaic of innumerable lakes, while the basin of the Great Lakes and the St Lawrence provide the greatest concentration of fresh water anywhere on earth, covering an area of 95,000 square miles. Ontario has 2,300 miles of freshwater shore on the Great Lakes and 700 miles of saltwater shore on Hudson and James Bays.

To give the European angler some idea of the distances involved, it is 2,000 miles from London to St Johns, Newfoundland, and it is 4,000 miles from St Johns to Victoria, British Columbia. For the sea angler the oceans provide tremendous sport, the west coast having 17,000 miles of coastline, and the eastern mainland alone, 6,000 miles.

In the northern regions, during the short summer season, the river estuaries are the haunt of the Arctic char; the western streams are the breeding grounds of the Pacific strains of salmon which provide the fisherman near the sea with year-round fishing. Chinook (king or tyee), coho (silver) are the two sport fish for the angler, while the smaller sockeye, dog and humpback are the species that the commercial netters harvest. The west is also the domain of the rainbow trout known as the 'steelhead', and the east coast rivers are the summer habitat of the spawning Atlantic salmon.

It is interesting to note that whereas the Atlantic salmon can spawn and return to the sea, the Pacific breeds die after propagating their species.

Angling for Canadian Atlantic salmon is done by fly fishing only, and it was here that the hairwing fly patterns were developed. A single-handed, 9ft rod anywhere from line class 7–10 is favoured for this type of fishing by the majority of North American anglers, although the traditional two-hand rod is still preferred by many when the fishing is done from a canoe. The flies used range from 3/0 to 10, and the Canadian salmon, unlike its European

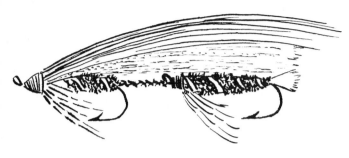

The 'George River' salmon streamer fly

Eastern steelhead nymph

Western trout nymph

cousin, is an eager taker of a feathered offering and dry fly is often employed to take them.

Char fishing is done mostly with spinning equipment: rods $6\frac{1}{2}$–$7\frac{1}{2}$ft, of sufficient power to cast $\frac{1}{4}$–$\frac{1}{2}$ ounce baits, are paired with reels loaded with 8–15lb test line, and red and white spoons are standard terminal equipment.

The most popular method for angling for the Pacific salmon breeds is a style called 'mooching'. Originally this method of angling appertained to saltwater fishing and related to a boat anchored in the tidal flow, and the half herring used as bait was allowed to flutter in the current. Done in a river, mooching is the Canadian version of the technique used on the Tay in Scotland, known as 'harling'. Nowadays in North America, however, the term mooching is applied to salmon fishing generally on the west coast.

The tackle used for this style of fishing consists of either a single action centre-pin reel, like a Hardy Silex, Young's Landex, or a multiplier such as the Ambassadeur 7000, loaded with at least 200 yards of

18–25lb test line, crescent-shaped lead weights, and a rod 9–10ft long with a pronounced fly rod action – in appearance, very similar to a British light saltwater bass rod, fitted with a fixed reel seat in a central-to-low position on the handle.

Trolling, and spincasting, spinning and baitcasting with large hairwing flies, spoons and spinners are all proven methods of taking Pacific salmon, and the light boat fishing tackle used on the Kent coast or off Plymouth would not be out of place in Cowichan Bay.

The steelhead is given top honours by the anglers west of the Rocky Mountains, and its fight is rated above even the chinook or the silver salmon. Regardless of angling method, it is essential to have a minimum of 200 yards of line on a reel that is mechanically sound, and a quality rod with lots of backbone. Steelhead are taken on a wide variety of baits and by many angling styles, but all require the bait to be fished close to the stream bottom, and the bait presented 'on the nose of the fish'.

The acceptance of the lure, although occasionally

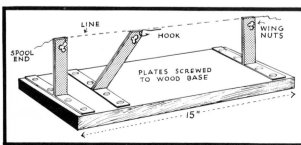

TOP TIP

It takes an expert to whip small hooks to nylon securely. This gadget makes it easy. Don't forget to add a dab of nail varnish to whippings, and tidy the loose ends of nylon by using nail clippers.

Eastern trout nymph

The 'Rusty Rat', one of the most popular salmon flies in Canada

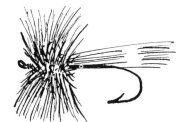

West Coast steelhead fly

Canadian Atlantic salmon dry fly

the classic, rod-arching, wrist-jolting, breath-catching, heart-skipping, smashing strike, is more often than not only a halting of the line, similar to the previous score or more of snags which such deeply-fished lures encounter (the most successful anglers say that unless the spoon is felt to bounce on the rocks there is little hope of a take). However when the line is tightened, if the bait has been taken by a steelhead, there is an electrifying contest ahead, with a fish that is rated pound for pound at the top of the piscine fighting scale.

It is a fish with amazing speed, fast enough to test the drag of the finest reel, with dogged strength plus fantastic stamina that put the best of equipment on trial, and a store of explosive energy that only a skilful angler armed with adequate tackle can battle.

There are two methods of steelhead angling that are worthy of more detailed explanation of interest to the European fisherman. 'Drifting' is a technique similar to the 'running the worm' method used in the North of England and Scotland, though the baits used in Canada are entirely different. Small sacks of salmon eggs – 'roe bags' – red or orange foam rubber balls, and scarlet or flame fluorescent yarn are all successfully employed to induce a take by this style of angling. The other method, 'stream mooching', is done by feeding the bait a foot or so at a time with the flow, every few seconds, which covers the section of the river below the angler thoroughly. Bait hooks used for this angling method are the stout wire, short shank variety, and the sinker weight used for this style of fishing is suspended from

a dropper of a much lower test than the main line (to eliminate excessive terminal tackle losses) positioned 2ft above the bait, and lead wire is often used – pencil leads as they are called, because of the shape of the weight – to avoid snagging between rocks.

Fly fishing is a popular approach to steelhead angling, the flies being extremely gaudy, and the accepted method is to fish them deeply sunk. Because of the wide rivers and the enormous volume of water flow, sinking shooting head lines are the standard equipment, paired with single-handed rods that will cast flies between size 2–10, and a fly reel with a good drag that has storage space for 200 yards of backing is an essential requirement.

Two other fish that are worthy of mention, found in the Rocky Mountain streams and on the west coast of Canada, are the Dolly Varden and cutthroat trouts. But it must be repeated that the rainbow – either migratory or landlocked – gets pride of place. Moving to the east of the Rockies, Northern pike are the main quarry of the angler, and to the far north there is trophy lake trout, grayling and brook trout fishing accessible only by float-fitted aircraft. The northern area contains Great Bear and Great Slave Lakes (both of which are strictly fly-in venues) and offer superb lake trout, grayling and pike angling, and where the shores of the Arctic touch these northlands there is truly fantastic char fishing.

East of the Great Slave Lake, walleye (a pike-perch similar in appearance to the zander) is added to the range of species, and as the Great Lakes Basin

TEACH-IN
on the art of fly-tying

IN fly-tying, remember that the exact imitations of insects have six legs, and spiders have eight. The stages are eggs to wingless nymphs, and then adults with one or two pairs of wings. Stone flies have two tails, and mayflies three.

A simple magnifying glass is sufficient to identify flies which are picked off the water by hand. Pond hunting is fascinating even to the non-specialist. Use an ordinary landing-net frame covered with fine muslin or an old silk headscarf.

Cut off the bottom corner to make a triangle and fit it into the neck of a screw-top jar. Examine the contents at home under a microscope.

DRAWING A shows the surplus herl trimmed, and the silk being wound towards the eye of the hook.

DRAWING B explains the technique of building up the body. A twist of the finger and thumb is given to the herl as it is wrapped around the hook shank.

After the body is formed as in DRAWING C, the herl is tied in. Careless and untidy winding will distort the fibres, so keep all the threads tight and ensure that the turns are straight, close and even. Slackness at any stage will cause the body to twist, and the hackle fibres will end up anywhere but in the right direction and the work is ruined.

Keep the work at eye level rather than looking down on it.

and St Lawrence is approached, bass, muskellunge, perch and pickerel supplement still further the Canadian angler's choice of quarry, with brook, brown and rainbow trout giving more zest to the angling scene.

The Great Lakes were once the domain of the lake trout. However, the vast stocks of these large, slow-growing members of the char family were almost completely decimated by the sea lamprey after the Welland Canal made the Great Lakes accessible from the ocean where, previously, the Niagara Falls had been an impassable barrier. During the past decade vigorous efforts have been made by the Fishery Departments of both the USA and Canada to control the lamprey menace, and by the electrical shock treatment of the breeding grounds of the creature (muddy-bottomed areas of feeder streams) there has been a drastic reduction in the numbers of this parasite. Determined attempts are now being made by both countries to restock the Great Lakes with lake trout.

Rainbow trout were introduced into the Great Lakes system in the early 1900s, and the strong migratory instincts of these species provide excellent spring and autumn fishing, in and around the spawning rivers which drain into the lakes. A small population of migratory brown trout (immigrants that arrived in Canada at the turn of the century) supply a further dash of flavour to the fishing; Coho salmon have been introduced into the Great Lakes over the past few years; kokanee (a small Pacific salmon), and a hybrid type splake (a cross between the speckled brook trout and the lake trout), have also been planted, and all have adapted well to the drainage basin area. There is an abundance of carp

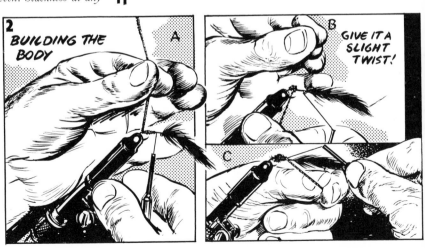

2 BUILDING THE BODY — A

GIVE IT A SLIGHT TWIST! — B

C

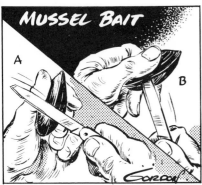
MUSSEL BAIT
A
B

C

13
D
PUT A
WORM
ON THE TIP
OF THE HOOK!
E

TEACH-IN... show 'em your mussels !

THE SEA is vast. Some fish are not so numerous, but mussels survive and multiply in great numbers. Harbour walls, rocks and inshore wreck-hulks ... all have their colony of mussels. The flesh of the mussel is an all-the-year-round bait, easy to preserve and equally easy to present to the fish.

DRAWING A: Scrape off the anchor threads to expose the opening for the foot of the mussel.

DRAWING B: Insert the point of the knife and twist; then slide the blade around the inside of the rim.

DRAWING C: All the flesh, including the 'mantle' rim,

is removed and put on the hook.

DRAWING D: Much of the flesh is soft and soon washes free. Strands of sheep's wool are used to keep it firm. By adding a worm to the 'tongue' of the mussel which is over the hook barb, we have a 'cocktail bait' which remains secure.

DRAWING E: Prawns must be put on the hook tail first, with whiskers intact. Haddock, gurnard, red bream, codling and flounders all take to the prawn like a country boy falling for Marilyn Monroe, but the wrasse, above all fish, is a prawn addict.

and suckers – a barbel-type family of fishes – which are virtually ignored by the North American anglers who concentrate their efforts on the game-fish types.

The muskellunge are the largest of the North American pike and have a dedicated following of fishermen who specialise in angling for them with huge 9–12in plugs, extra-large spoons and dead baits over 1ft in length. Stout baitcasting reels, strong rods and 30lb test line are employed when an angler tries to induce a strike from these cautious, solitary monsters that reach weights exceeding 60lb and fight like tarpon.

Tackle requirements to cover most of the general angling situations in Canada consist of a spinning or spincast rod, 6–7ft long, strong enough to cast lures from $\frac{1}{4}$–$\frac{1}{2}$oz, paired with a reel, either closed face or open, loaded with line from 8–12lb test.

Bass, pike and walleye are taken on plugs, spoons

and swinging blade spinners as well as natural baits, such as minnows, leeches, frogs and earth worms. A terminal tackle rig that is essentially North American is to see a spoon such as a Mepps, with the treble hook draped with dew worms. Another type of lure, particular to Canadian angling, is the 'jig', a hook with an off-set eye, fitted with a lead head, and a skirt of either hair or feathers (which is a lure that produces a terrific action). It is a proven taker of predatory fish when jigged tantalisingly through the water, while the skills of anglers using plastic worms and other rubber-like creations that have tails that wag, vibrate and flutter account for a fair percentage of fish brought to the net. Plug baits such as the Rapala and Rebel which represent minnows, and those that create surface disturbance or set up underwater vibrations – poppers, crawlers, wrigglers, darters, divers and deep runners – are

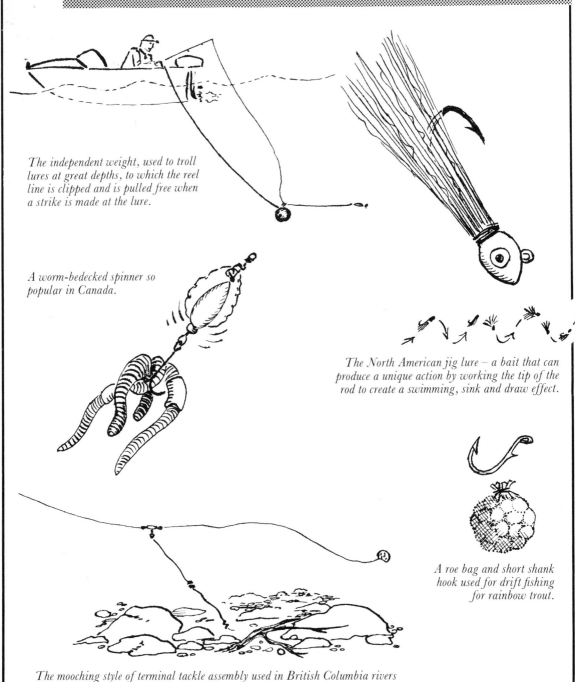

The independent weight, used to troll lures at great depths, to which the reel line is clipped and is pulled free when a strike is made at the lure.

A worm-bedecked spinner so popular in Canada.

The North American jig lure – a bait that can produce a unique action by working the tip of the rod to create a swimming, sink and draw effect.

A roe bag and short shank hook used for drift fishing for rainbow trout.

The mooching style of terminal tackle assembly used in British Columbia rivers (note lead wire weight).

88

used with great success and all have their advocates.

Trout (brown, rainbow and brook), bass and pike provide excellent sport for the fly fisherman, with nymphs, wet flies, streamers, dry flies and cork or deer-hair floating lures being employed to catch their quarry.

Great Lake coho salmon show a preference for red fluorescent-coloured lures, although once the spawning instinct prevails, they show little interest in the angler's lure. To take advantage of such a marvellous sport fish, however, deep-water trolling techniques are being developed, and off-shore rigs that employ a heavy lead weight sunk at a depth of 50ft or more on an independent line, to which the line is clipped. A strike pulls the line free, and the fish is played from the rod and reel, and in open water, tests of 6–8lb can be used to defeat fish over 30lb.

For the migratory rainbow of the Great Lakes Basin, a medium-sized swinging blade spinner is a very popular lure, although drifting bags of roe is possibly the most favoured angling method. Cheese, corn, marshmallows and $\frac{1}{2}$in yellow, red and orange foam-rubber balls are also used for this style of fishing. Rods similar to those employed for European carp or barbel fishing are used for drift fishing – a style reminiscent in both terminal tackle assembly and application to that of the upstream worm method in the North of England. In Canada a single, short shank hook is invariably used for rainbow, while long shank hooks are favoured for the sharp-toothed species such as bass and walleye.

Lake trout are caught mainly by trolling, and

either wire lines or those of the braided, lead centre type are necessary to reach the depths at which these fish are found. Terminal rigs consist of a series of spinning blades on a 2–4ft wire leader, on to which a 4–8in spoon is attached. The largest 'laker' to be recorded weighed over 100lb and was caught by commercial netters.

The areas that offer the quality of fishing seen in glossy magazines can only be reached by aeroplane, and the short summer angling season of the far north places further limitations on the accessibility of such places, and climatic conditions must also be considered. Fishing the Great Bear Lake even at the height of the summer season finds the water temperature so low that an angler tumbling into the lake is able to survive only for a matter of minutes because it is so cold. In wilderness areas that are frozen for the greater part of the year, the summer transforms them into insect-infested lands that test the tenacity of the most ardent angler. And wilderness means *WILDERNESS*, with the bulk of the perimeter of lakes an impenetrable mass of deadfalls and trees (canoes are flown in), and streams are bordered by a tangled mass of undergrowth and forest; the tundra lands which border the Arctic are open, but down-filled clothing is a must, even during the summer.

A great part of Canada lies within the Arctic Circle, and the bulk of the population is distributed in a belt some 200 miles wide on the southern border. Canada, however, has within its boundaries more than 290,000 square miles of fresh water.

North America is the land of angling lures, and the selection of plug-types, spoon-shapes, spinners, jigs, trolls and flies, when computed with colours and materials (both natural and synthetic), is almost endless.

Flies, for example, range from 6in long, hair and hackle creations used for Pacific salmon in salt-water, to the minuscule No. 22 for taking the hyper-sophisticated eastern brown trout. Certain of the flies, which suggest Canadian bait fish or imitate

ANGLERS can now put a boat on top of the car and travel almost anywhere, but some foolishly risk their lives by putting out to sea without a spare can of petrol, oars and lifejackets (as in Picture A). However, the amateur boatmen have had the good manners to keep clear of the pier angler.

In Picture B, the 'three wise men' have done the right thing by evenly spreading out in the boat. They also carry smoke flares and have notified those on shore of the approximate time of return, so that if they do become overdue a search can be called.

When the tide-race is strong, follow the procedure shown in Picture C.

Teach-In on common sense

subaqueous creatures, are at times quite deadly, although the nymphs tied on size 4 hooks that are successful in the Rockies are reduced to size 16 in eastern Canada.

The North American patterns are different from the trout patterns of Europe, although there are of course similarities. For salmon fishing on the east coast, the traditional Scottish dressings of Jock Scott and Green Highlander rank close in popularity to the Canadian Rusty Rat and Black Dose, originated by J. C. Arsenault who is the father of the Canadian hairwing salmon fly. To the north, on the Ungava Bay rivers, the twin-hook, terror-type fly, tied with a moose beard wing, hauntingly resembles the Tweed Terror, developed by George Tait for the spring and fall salmon angling on the River Tweed.

Plugs over 1ft in length are at the base of a size pyramid topped by minute, quarter-inch fly rod creations. Eight-inch spoons lead an innumerable array of hardware, terminated with tiny slivers of metal that take fish through holes cut in the ice covering lakes during the Canadian winter. Red and white combinations are the predominant colour schemes, followed by black and yellow, and orange and brown, while silver is more popular than gold in metallic finishes.

The fabulous speckled brook trout of Quebec, the princely Arctic char, the fantastic Labrador Atlantic salmon, the enormous lake trout of Great Bear, the tremendous steelhead of British Columbia, or the splendid grayling of the North-West Territories are placed well beyond the points where logging roads end, and where the untouched wilderness remains the access is by float plane only.

The north lands are magnificently wild, stark and cruel, as natural today as they were 2,000 years ago . . . where a river that can provide unbelievable fishing to a skilled angler in the lee of an island, will crush a canoe and attempt to snatch the life of an unwary soul at the very next rapid.

There are still places where the tundra moss is 6in thick and will retain footprints for decades . . . where stunted trees scarcely 20ft tall are centuries old . . . where the water is so clean and clear that pebbles radiate pure colours hardly possible to comprehend . . . where deer and beaver will captivate the angler – and the approach of a bear or moose causes the spot to be hastily evacuated by the fisherman . . . where stars twinkle from a black velvet sky and wolves still howl to the moon . . .

Canada is a land of vast distances, but within its confines it contains what must surely be the finest assortment of fishing in the most natural, exquisite settings to be found anywhere in the world.

HOW TO BEAT THE MONSTER!

MARINE eels, denizens of the deep, put the fear of Old Nick into unsuspecting anglers.

If a conger takes the bait intended for a lesser fish, panic-stricken fishermen hurriedly cut the line and breathe a sigh of relief as the fish goes free.

A conger of any weight fights well. The one below (bottom right) turned the scales at 53lb.

As congers are selective feeders, fresh bait is a must. Whole fillet of fish are swallowed head first. The hook (top left) should be crimped

to a stainless steel wire trace.

When the fish is on the hook, get it up and off the bottom as quickly as possible, otherwise the monster will find a secure lair and anchor from which it will never let go.

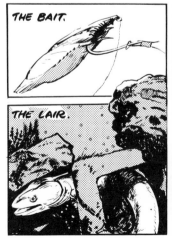

THE BAIT.

THE LAIR.

ON THE HOOK.

GORDON

This eel weighed a mere 14lb, but it is a fine catch because on the day few fish were caught. The catch was made off Stornoway by a holiday angler from Kent.

WATCHDOGS

INTEREST in the sport of angling has increased by leaps and bounds over the past 20 years or so. Now it is estimated that more people go fishing on a Saturday in the coarse fishing season than go to watch all the matches in the four divisions of the Football League. In fact, angling has rapidly become the major participant sport in the British Isles.

In 1956, the total number of rod licences sold in the United Kingdom was slightly over 720,000; by 1973, the total figure was well over 1,250,000. There are also some areas where rod licences are not required and where, of course, there will be more anglers. Clubs have increased in numbers and angling organisation has strengthened all over the country.

Angling is also the most widely organised sport at all levels with national bodies for each branch – coarse, game and sea. In 1966, the Minister for Sport suggested to anglers that they should form one Council which could speak to him and The Sports Council and the Government on behalf of the sport. So it was that the National Anglers' Council was formed to represent all branches of the sport. Its activities are at the highest level.

In 1970 the Council published the National Angling Survey, the most comprehensive survey of the sport ever undertaken. It revealed that there were then 2,790,000 anglers, and that by 1980 this figure would reach 3,250,000. It gave information on club membership, cost of angling, frequency of fishing, preferred species and many other details. It has become the standard reference for the sport and its publication encouraged more commercial interest in angling, especially in sponsorship and news coverage by national and weekly newspapers.

The Council's main role in recent years has been that of 'watchdog' over any legislation which may affect angling or fisheries. Several important Acts of Parliament have been passed recently, notably the Salmon and Freshwater Fisheries Act (1972), the Water Act (1973) and the Control of Pollution Act (1974). These acts vitally affect the sport, as also does the 1968 Transport Act which included proposals for canals and inland waterways on which 250,000 anglers fish. The Council was successful in having fishing written into the Act and has secured three seats for angling on the Inland Waterways

by Peter Tombleson

PETER TOMBLESON has been secretary of the National Anglers' Council since 1967. A former journalist and founder staff member of *Angling Times* in 1953, he also founded the British Record (rod-caught) Fish Committee, of which he is secretary. He has written several angling books.

Amenity Advisory Council, which advises British Waterways Board on amenity proposals.

It is a prime task of the Council to ensure that wherever a committee or organisation's work may affect angling or fisheries, the angling voice is heard. But not all of the Council's activities are devoted to legislation. It gives advice on a wide range of problems affecting fishing clubs – rates, taxes, fishery management, legal problems, social activities, club regulations, and many more. The angling club secretary faced with a problem new to him or to his committee can seek and obtain advice from the Council.

In 1968 the Council, with the support of Player's No. 6 as sponsors, set up an Aid to Angling Fund which has distributed several thousand pounds in grants to angling clubs wishing to develop their facilities. The Council also advises clubs on Sports Council grants and has negotiated improvement of grant terms to meet the special needs of angling. As a result, more money has been made available to the sport.

A new development is the promotion of a National Coaching Scheme to ensure that newcomers to the sport can receive tuition through qualified instructors. It also has an information service for members and issues thousands of Newsletters and leaflets annually.

In addition to all this, the Council looks after British fish records and is responsible for the British Record (rod-caught) Fish Committee, which investigates claims for the largest species of fish caught in the British Isles.

Claims for a new record should be made to the Council Secretary, who is also the Committee Secretary. Instructions are then given for identification of the fish through Liverpool University, the Marine Biological Association or other academic institutions.

Once identification is proven, the claimant must complete claim forms obtaining the signatures of witnesses to the capture and to the weighing of the fish. A Weights and Measures Certificate for the scales used is essential, unless the fish is weighed on trade scales which are regularly tested officially. The claim forms go to the Committee, which meets twice a year and is made up of representatives of the national angling bodies, scientific members, the angling Press and periodicals, and representatives of Welsh and Scottish sea angling organisations. Each claim is considered on its merits, but the body of the fish is normally required.

When the Committee began in 1957 there were only about 50 species on the list. Now there are more than 100, the increase having come mainly from sea fish, and it is in the sea fish area where records change most frequently. Perhaps this is because sea fishing methods have improved rapidly over the past few years and a wider range of species is now caught.

There is more interest in record fish in the UK than in many European countries, but there is now a Dutch Sea Fish Record Committee and a Polish Record Fish Commission, both of which have based their methods of procedure on those of the British Record (rod-caught) Fish Committee. There are also separate record sea fish committees for Scotland and Wales.

HAVING FINGER TROUBLE?

Then here are two tips for you...

WHEN fingers are cold, hooks which hang straight instead of curling around the nylon are a blessing in disguise. Just slot them into an old cigar box (diagram on right), where they are ready to transfer to the business end of the line in seconds.

The other diagram shows you how to deal with rapidly-moving nylon that can cut through flesh as fast and neat as a razor cutting butter. Long-casting 'level' reels as used in sea fishing have to be braked with the thumb or the forefinger – and that's when anglers get burned and cut up. Solve the problem by attaching a leather key fob to the reel crossbar. It must be a leather fob with stitching. After the split ring is taken off, make a slot for the thumb. When reeling the line in, the fob is simply flipped back.

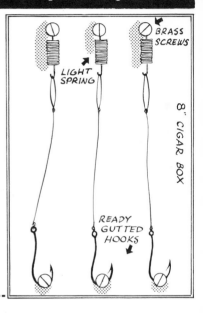

TEACH-IN on the changes in tackle

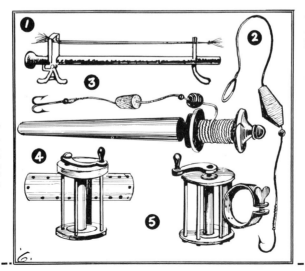

ARISTOCRATIC tackle in use today grew from crude beginnings. Seventeen centuries ago, early anglers knew that red wool and cock's feathers would excite and attract fish. But no dramatic advance was made until about the year 1500, when a 6ft rod (or pole) was used to dangle a line of equal length.

Lines were made of horsehair strands twisted together. It was fashioned on the type of machine shown in Picture 1. Legering was commonly indulged in, and the rig in

Picture 2 was a great success. Before the hook was invented, it was the practice to use a piece of shell or bone $1\frac{1}{2}$ ins long and sharpened at each end. It was buried in meat. When the fish gorged upon it, the unfortunate creature was smartly heaved out of the water.

Picture 3 shows a running hand-line. The two 18th-Century reels have different ratios. Figure 4 has a quicker retrieve than model 5, because the winding handle is in a different position.

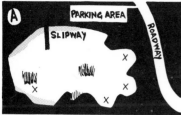

TEACH-IN on keeping records

NEVER TAKE a beaten fish for granted, and always use landing net (B) because even a tired fish will make a last-minute dash for freedom.

When sea fishing, make a recce at low tide (C) to find out what the fishing area looks like when covered with water. And when fishing among rocks and seaweed for flatties and codling, there is no harm in having a net handy to make sure of landing your catch. The net handle will serve as a wading stick to probe the dangerous crevices.

Most anglers keep an angling diary to record their catches, the weather, water conditions and baits used. But very few fishermen make an angling atlas of the places visited.

All waters have their secrets, such as where the underwater obstructions are, the best places to cast from, and the deepest holes which harbour fish. The information can be coded (Picture A) and the stored information put to good advantage next time the water is visited.

Teach-In on boat fishing

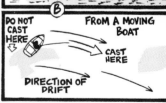

WHEN fishing from a boat, remember that a moving shadow will scare fish. So when lake fishing from an anchored boat, always keep the boat out of the sun by dropping anchor in the shade of a tree or under an overhanging bank. And when coming to anchor, never throw the weight over the side but lower it gently (Picture A). Clumsy movements in and around the boat could scare the fish off.

If the fishing is done from a moving boat, it is called 'fishing the drift', and the line should always be cast to where the boat is going and not to where it is coming from (Picture B).

Keep an eye open for minor explosions on the surface of the water (Picture C), which indicate that a hungry pike is driving into and feeding upon the shoals of smaller fish. The hungry pike wil readily take an angler's lure.

Random thoughts of a fly fishing historian

T. DONALD OVERFIELD was born in East Yorkshire, close by the famous chalk-stream at Driffield. His main angling interests are dry-fly and nymph. He writes and illustrates regularly for British, American and Swedish fishing journals, and is International Director of the Flyfishers Foundation. He has written books and was chosen as the historian to update that classic volume, 'A Dictionary of Trout Flies'.

by T. DONALD OVERFIELD

JUST where does one's interest in the past begin? For myself I must confess to a lifelong love of history. While at school I preferred the Romans to rugby, the Celts to cricket, to the annoyance of some who would have had me pounding after a muddy ball or attempting a mighty hook over square-leg. Such pursuits had a certain interest for me and I was not entirely discredited when

handling a ball, be it large or small. However, the thoughts of a 'dig' in some Anglo-Saxon barrow raised my blood pressure more than a trip to Twickenham or Lord's.

This interest in the past has not blinkered me to the advantages of the present day. A medieval castle can certainly be improved for comfort by the installation of central heating, in the same way that a modern fibreglass rod can out-perform the old lance-wood creation. But the fibreglass rod could not have existed without the transition from lance-wood, through greenheart and bamboo, and there is the fascination that can provide countless years of study. The same can be said of the evolution of the trout and salmon fly.

Early investigation of the history of fly tying teaches one to suspect some statements in print, and there lies the fascination of detective work and miles of travelling to ascertain facts. Take, for example, the history of that well-known North-country fly, the John Storey, which has been accredited to three different sources – a gamekeeper with the Earl of Feversham (circa 1880), an unknown angler on the Yorkshire Derwent (1901) and John Storey, river-keeper to Ryedale Angling Club (1911). I have also seen variations of the pattern called John Storey, so I determined to discover the facts of both the true dressing and the originator.

I started my search in the area of the River Rye in North Yorkshire and my first call was at the Black Swan, Helmesley, through which the river runs. I learned that a Storey could still be found in the town, and soon I was with Arthur Storey, the head river keeper for the Ryedale Club, in his trim stone cottage.

The unknown Derwent angler theory was soon discounted, but the two remaining theories were, in part, correct. John Storey had worked for Lord Feversham before becoming the river keeper in 1857. Storey was born at Nunnington, four miles from Helmesley, in 1834, and the pattern that bears

his name was invented shortly after he became keeper. The fly was, of course, a wet pattern, size 14, tied to gut. It had an underbody of fawn wool, overlaid with copper-coloured peacock herl. The hackle was a sparsely-applied Rhode Island red, while the wing was a bunched mallard breast feather sloping back over the body.

In 1914 John Storey died and his son, Herbert, took over. The fly underwent a design change in the period 1915–1920, when the new keeper dressed it as a dry fly. He deleted the fawn underbody, substituted a high-grade cock hackle of the same colour, but used more turns as an aid to floatation, while the wings were brought upright in the manner of a typical dry fly. He continued to tie the wet version as well as the dry, but the latter became highly popular and a proven fish-taker.

Herbert Storey died in 1932, when the keepership passed to his brother, who was already 63. He died in 1941 and his widow Hannah became river-keeper until Arthur Storey returned from the war in 1945, at the age of 25.

Now to the point of great interest to the fly tyer. Just when did the pattern evolve from the usual upright, winged, dry style to the form known to anglers today, with the wings sloping at an acute angle over the eye? The answer is 1935. I have heard many theories bandied about regarding the wing formation, and some of them highly complex. The simple truth is that, in 1935, the present keeper was learning to tie flies and experienced great difficulty in the normal form of dry-fly winging. As an experiment, he dressed dry flies with the forward

TEACH-IN ON FLY BOXES

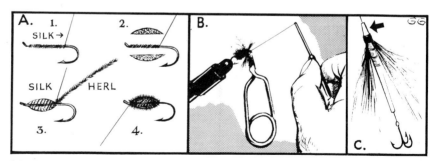

AS trout season ends, many river fishermen will be replenishing their fly boxes throughout the winter evenings. Picture A shows how to make a full-bodied Coachman Fly which is unsinkable.

Stage 1) Cover the hook shank with silk. 2) Tie in two cigar-shaped pieces of polystyrene which can be cut from ceiling tiles. 3) Cover with ostrich herl and trim as at Stage

4, then just add the wings and hackle in the usual way.

Picture B illustrates the method of hackle tying. And C shows a comparative newcomer in flies – the Tube Fly. The nose-cone (arrowed) is made of brass or lead to allow the fly to fish well down. The nylon to the tail-end treble hook passes through the body of the tube.

Arthur Storey in action. He is the present-day keeper on the Rye and the originator of the forward-wing 'John Storey'.

sloping wing. These were tried by his father and members of the club and for no truly accountable reason they were highly successful. Since that time, all John Storey patterns have been tied that way.

The fly has also been the subject of much speculation as to what it represents. The simple fact is that it was never intended to represent any natural fly. It is simply a general purpose pattern.

My visit to Helmesley also confirmed the true present-day pattern of the John Storey. It is tied upon a No. 14 D/E hook. The silk is black. Tails are not fitted, neither is a rib. The body is copper-coloured peacock herl, while the hackle is a Rhode Island Red cock. The wings are of a small breast feather, whole, from the mallard, taken from the adult bird. The feathers of young birds should not be used because of their brownish tinge.

To some it may appear that I am making much of a trifle. However, the following has been established: (1) The name, date of birth and death of the inventor; (2) Approximate date of the original pattern; (3) The original, and subsequent, dressing; (4) The correct present-day dressing. Would that it were possible to do the same with countless other patterns!

To complete a project so easily is not usually the lot of the fly fishing historian. It is the incomplete story, the unfound vital clue, that keeps one looking, reading and searching.

When researching my book *Famous Flies and their Originators*, I thought that the chapter on James Wright, the Sprouston fly dresser who first 'busked' the Greenwell's Glory, would present few problems. Didn't we all know that the pattern was devised from an unnamed natural fly brought to Wright on that famous day in May 1854 by Canon William Greenwell, and how the following day the worthy cleric went to the Tweed to test the new pattern, returning with a basket of trout? The story is known to all fly fishers, I'm sure.

As I delved into the past, a doubt crossed my mind. Was the fly we know as the Greenwell's Glory truly the invention of James Wright, or did he pass on to the canon a pattern already used on the Tweed? A letter from the canon on June 1, 1900 gave the dressing as being on a No. 14 hook, yellow silk, the wings of a feather taken from the inside of a blackbird's wing, while the hackle was a coch-y-bondhhu. It is generally agreed that Greenwell later confirmed that the silk should be given a 'greenish hue' by the application of cobbler's wax, and that a gold rib may be added. The dressing so described is

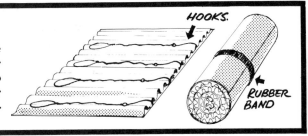

TOP TIP

All anglers welcome 'tidy tips' because the tackle box quickly becomes a hold-all for a mixture of small bits and pieces. A strip of corrugated cardboard is first-class for keeping snoods and hooks readily available.

HOOKS.

RUBBER BAND

accepted as the true and authentic Greenwell's Glory.

Now we turn to a book not known to many fly fishers – Ewen M. Tod's *Wet Fly Fishing*, published in 1903. It contains many references and much praise for the fly-tying ability of Mark Aitkin, a regular angler on the Tweed. It becomes obvious that Aitkin was many years senior to Tod and must have been his mentor in the craft of tying the artificial fly. Tod lists many of Aitkin's fly patterns and one, number VIII, tells us that the body is of yellow waxed silk, the wing from the inside feather of a blackbird wing while the hackle is a coch-y-bondhu, or black.

Could it be that the celebrated Greenwell's Glory was not, after all, a new pattern on that May day in 1854? Did James Wright dress for the canon a pattern already well known on the Tweed, or did Wright beat Aitkin by a short head and the latter included Wright's pattern under the number VIII? It is interesting, but confusing, to note that the rib is missing in Aitkin's dressing, as it was in the canon's original letter.

So many questions remain unanswered and will continue to provide material in all facets of fly fishing. The written word of our chosen sport can be traced back to the Third Century and to Claudius Aelianus when he described the artificial fly with which the Macedonians tempted the 'spotted fish' (surely trout?). Aelianus tells us that 'round the hook they twist scarlet wool and two wings are secured on this wool from the feathers that grow under the wattles of a cock, brought to the proper colour with wax.'

How I, and many others, would love to know the configuration of such a pattern! The wings

TEACH-IN on the FLY CREATURES

FLY FISHING rods are light, lively and sensitive. Anglers use them as wands to drop the gossamer fly to a waiting trout. In spate water, and when fishing for salmon, the heavier flies are worked through the pools to imitate the flitting and darting movement of hatching insects or small fish. Small fry are easy prey and a favourite food for cannibal fish.

A Tube fly has a detachable metal body. It is fitted with a lead nose-cone to prevent it 'skating' over the water. The wet fly is fished at various depths, but the dry fly is presented on the surface. The baits which are specifically designed to represent small fish are called lures. But they are given the trappings of a fly.

The structure for an artificial fly is shown on the bottom-left of the first picture. A – Wing, B – Body, C – Tail, D – Tag, E – Butt, F – Hackle, G – Head.

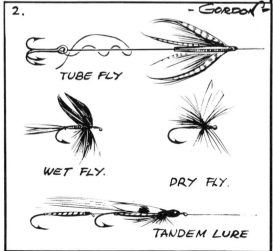

Overfield on a favourite beat.

especially provide for intriguing thought. Were they of hook length? At what angle were they set upon the hook? Were they possibly like a streamer? This must be one question that no historian can answer. The mists of time have fully covered the facts and we have no other source material from which to make deductions.

All thinking fly fishers must wish that facts, and yet more facts, be clearly set down in this present day so that future fly fishing historians will have a less arduous task. Somehow I doubt if it will happen. Take, for example, that excellent pattern devised by the late Oliver Kite in 1962, the Imperial, his representation of the male large olive dun. Already it is being bastardised by fly tyers who should know better. Recent angling Press comments have given it a body of peacock herl, and even black ostrich herl, when it should be of undyed heron herl.

I fear that the historian of the year 2500 is going to have just the same problems as his present-day counterparts. At least he may be spared the need to fish occasionally, for I am sure that our beloved sport will have long since passed into the realms of antiquity and even the fly fisher himself may be the subject of investigation by some socialogically-inclined historian!

TEACH-IN on how to be a fly man

MOST artificial flies used by anglers are so dainty and pretty that they catch more fishermen than fish. The more ragged and tattered a fly becomes, the more likely it is to appeal to fish.

'*My best fish-catching flies were tied at the water's edge*', *says Charles Wade.* '*They were constructed from bits of moss plus wool strands from whatever pullover I happened to have on at the time.*'

The late Oliver Kite, a famous chalk-stream trout angler, used to fish with a 'fly' that just resembled a bit of stick. But he also designed a very famous fly that went under the name of Kite's Imperial. You can tie a Kite's Imperial by following the various stages as shown in Picture A.

A fly fisherman gains enormous help from wearing the waistcoat in Picture B. It has loads of pockets and clips and belts. The whole thing just slips on top of the angler's normal clothes.

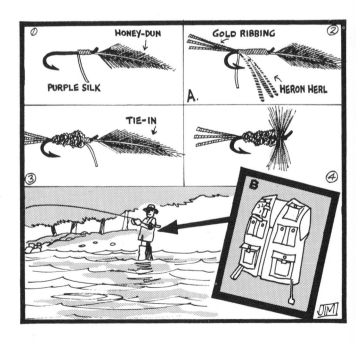

MOMENT of TRUTH

This is the moment of a strike ... and the angler's moment of truth. Fishing fine and far off, the strike has to be firm – but not too hard. This may break the line.

IT'S IN THE BAG!

There's no escape for this trout taken on a nymph by Harvey Torbett at Blagdon Lake.

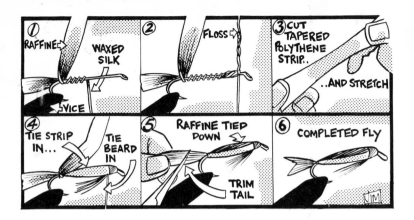

1. RAFFINE → WAXED SILK ← VICE
2. FLOSS →
3. CUT TAPERED POLYTHENE STRIP.. ...AND STRETCH
4. TIE STRIP IN... TIE BEARD IN
5. RAFFINE TIED DOWN TRIM TAIL
6. COMPLETED FLY

JIM

TEACH-IN on fly minnows

KEEPING pace with the improving methods of angling, the tackle we use must also be updated. Here we see the old-time fly minnow, which was used 40 years ago, appearing now in a new dress and called the Polystickle. It is easy to make.

Use a white hook in preference to a bronzed one. Tease the floss out (Picture 2) with finger and thumb

before tying-in. Choose green, olive blue or a mixture of these colours for the polythene (raffine) and stretch as in Picture 3.

The completed fly (Picture 6) is meant to imitate a small fish, and in use the line should be retrieved smartly in short six-inch jerks to make the lure swim correctly.

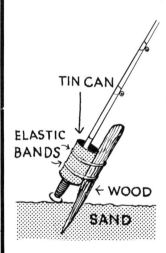
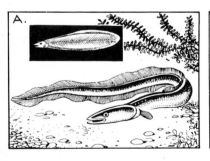

A.

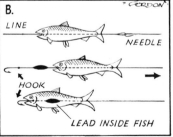

B.

GORDON

LINE
NEEDLE
HOOK
LEAD INSIDE FISH

EELS start out in life as larvae which are practically transparent and leaf-shaped, as in Picture A (top left). Female eels of 3ft long are fairly common. The male eel rarely exceeds 20in.

Eels hide in holes or beneath stones and rocks in the daytime.

Teach-In on eels

They come out to feed, chiefly at night. Larger eels will eat almost anything, including

birds, frogs and voles. They can travel across damp soil and wet grass.

Some anglers fish with a ball of red wool tangled in short strands. The eel hangs on by the teeth. But the best method is to use a dead minnow baited as shown in Picture B.

TEACH-IN ON FLY FISHING

WHEN fly fishing, the rod is simply an extension of the shoulder, arm and wrist. Pictures 1 and 2 show the rod in action.

In dry-fly angling, the fish takes the insect from the top of the water. The artificial lure should represent an agile fly busily laying a batch of eggs. It can also imitate an exhausted moth or a bee blown down by a gust of wind.

1.   2.

A purist dry-fly fisherman will rigidly use a single fly and he will always cast upstream. The movements and stance for this activity are shown in the middle picture, where the angler is placing a fly to a fish which is close to the bank.

Wet flies are fished below the surface and they imitate a fully-formed insect rising to take wing after being hatched under water.

The bottom picture shows a wet-fly cast. Sometimes a third 'dropper' is added and it is called the 'bob' fly because it flutters on the surface while the others are sunken. A cast is usually about 7ft 6in long and the flies are spaced from the tail (or point) at 18-inch intervals.

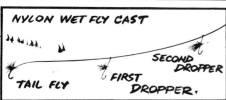

DRY FLY FISHING

FLOW

NYLON WET FLY CAST

SECOND DROPPER

TAIL FLY   FIRST DROPPER.

Here's a tidy tip

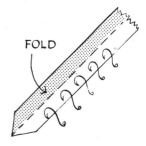

FOLD

To carry hooks safely and tidily, place them on a folded Sellotape strip, but keep the eyes of the hooks uppermost. At the riverside, when a new hook is needed, tie it first and then snip off from the folded strip.

Teach-In on knots

THREE knots illustrated below should be mastered before trying for trout: A) The clinch knot is used for tying a swivel, B) The blood knot is used for joining together two pieces of nylon, C) A turle knot is used for tying the line to the fly.

Nothing sets the angler's blood tingling faster than the rise of a trout to a fly (Picture A). Sometimes the rise is called an 'explosion' (Picture B). But when the trout is merely sucking in the flies from the film on the surface of the water (Picture C), the term is 'dimpling'.

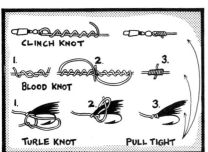

CLINCH KNOT
1.   2.   3.
BLOOD KNOT
1.   2.   3.
TURLE KNOT   PULL TIGHT

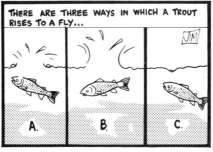

THERE ARE THREE WAYS IN WHICH A TROUT RISES TO A FLY...

A.   B.   C.

Beachcasting rods...

BY

JOHN HOLDEN

COMPLICATION is often the by-product of progress. Take shorecasting rods as an example. Back in the old days, before fibreglass, the most common rod was a Burma cane. Burma canes are long, strong and inflexible. True, they cast heavy weights and quell big fish, but they were heavy and clumsy.

As sea fishing became less a food-gathering exercise and more of a sport, sophistication followed. The trusty Burma cane was upstaged, first by cut-down salmon rods and built-cane beachcasters, then by fibreglass. The original fibreglass rods were no more than synthetic Burma canes. There wasn't the know-how to design anything better; and anyway, what was wrong with the canes? Or so asked the rod makers.

While the tackle industry laboured in their ivory towers, sea anglers started thinking. Leslie Moncrieff showed what could be done with properly designed rods, in his case the Springheel reversed-taper rod. At a time when most anglers threw 50 yards, Leslie cast 150. He caught more fish by doing so; the Dungeness cod hauls are almost legendary.

Tournament casting grew up, or more correctly was reborn, from long-range beachcasting. By the late 1960s, some casters had bettered 200 yards with more or less standard fishing tackle and 6oz leads. But the tail began to wag the dog. Tournament tackle and techniques began to filter from the courts to the shore. Some rods were de-tuned from full competitive order to better suit fishing. Many manufacturers sold beach rods almost entirely on the strength of their tournament performances.

In fact, of course, it was the caster who made the rod, not vice versa. In a few cases, especially with fast-tapered rods, special casting styles had to be invented to extract the ultimate distances so necessary to win at a tournament. Naturally, perhaps, those same styles found their way to the beach and into the hands of the average angler. The classic

example is the Pendulum cast with its long, vicious power stroke and initial lead swinging. It is very dangerous.

The average angler is a poor caster. He cannot understand and properly perform Moncrieff's simple Layback. On a crowded beach, his fumbling with fast rod and Pendulum cast is potentially lethal – already, near fatal accidents have occurred.

We must have a return to simplicity; to rods and reels of adequate performance which can be

the future

Long-distance casts are helped by being above the water line and this bait soared over 100 yards into the surf during a match at Folkestone – the All-England beach and European championship fished by more than 1,500 anglers.

powered by safe, easy casts. Two years ago, that would have been a pipedream, but today it is very much on the cards. For fast-tapered rods and associated casts are on the wane. The tackle is already outclassed on the tournament field.

In the 1973 World Casting Championships, the South Africans thrashed us, fast-tapered rods and all. They use basic off-the-ground casts and long, medium speed rods. Already some of our top casters have made the change. And already distances are

creeping up: in 1974, Terry Carroll set a new British 6oz record of 222 yards. Up in Suffolk, Nigel Forrest, undisputedly our best casting technician, is working on African-style rods.

It is now only a matter of time until the African cast and tackle come to our beaches. Their offer of simple casting to extreme range is too important to be overlooked for long. Again, as with fast rods and Pendulum casts, the tournament tail will wag the beach dog. But this time, for the better.

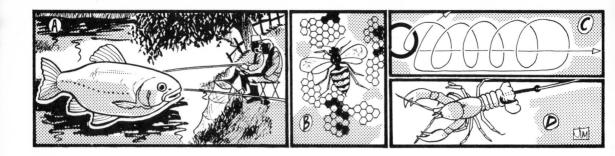

Teach-In on chub

CHUB (A), which are widely distributed fish, are cunning, wary and, at times, very gluttonous. They possess powerful shoulders and a strong, heavy body.

They are often found under overhanging branches, close to steep walls and beneath bridges, or near to reed beds. They will run for cover to deep holes if the angler betrays his presence.

Wasp cake and wasp grubs (B) are a superb bait for chub. They will also fall for a crayfish providing it is mounted correctly on the hook (D).

Strong tackle and secure knots are essential when chub fishing. The four-fold blood knot (C) is tucked at the end to secure hooks and swivels adequately.

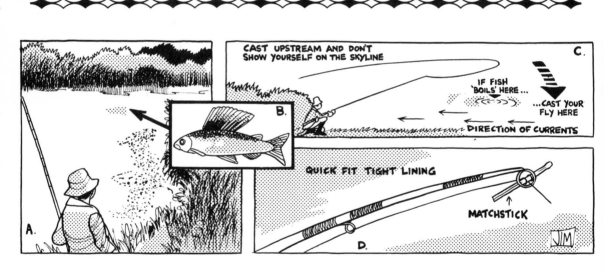

CAST UPSTREAM AND DON'T SHOW YOURSELF ON THE SKYLINE

C.

IF FISH 'BOILS' HERE ...

...CAST YOUR FLY HERE

DIRECTION OF CURRENTS

QUICK FIT TIGHT LINING

MATCHSTICK

FROSTY days and nights suit the grayling. It is a hard fish unaffected by the coldness of the water. And when the line freezes to the rod rings, the angler can expect super sport.

Look for Madam Grayling where the water runs at a leisured pace (Picture A), and preferably over mud and clay. And be prepared when the hooked fish takes off with a rush. The sail-like fin (Picture B) gives the fish tremendous power.

Grubs, worms and flies – and occasionally spinners – will

Teach-In on grayling

take fish. When float fishing, manipulate the line so that the bait searches and 'trots' downstream (Picture C).

Use a fly that has some red and some silver in its make-up. To fish with a tight line when after bleak, gudgeon or minnows for grayling bait, use a matchstick fitting (Picture D).

GEOFFREY BUCKNALL

GEOFFREY BUCKNALL has gathered a wealth of angling experience in 30 years' fishing. Although he specialises in fly fishing for trout, he is an all-round angler. Geoff has a busy angling life. He is a Council member of the ACA, Vice-President of the Fly-Tyers Guild, Chairman of the Southern Casting Association and a member of Bromley AA, Tonbridge AA and Canterbury AA. He runs a tackle shop and a wholesale and tackle manufacturing business. This gives him the opportunity to design and manufacture rods of his specification. He has written seven angling books and has created his own trout fishery at Sundridge, Kent.

New aspects on still water trouting

STILL-WATER fly fishing is exciting because it is in a state of growth – almost explosion. New ideas on tackle, flies and methods of fishing are being used, often experimentally, and I am trying to trace this evolution in such a way as to single out the most valuable elements.

Take the rod itself. We marched into the fifties armed with the theory of the long, slow fly rod which only a giant could flex. One of these was well named 'the Iron Murderer', a most beautiful object in 10ft of dark, glistening split cane. It typified the fallacy of the time, that distance casting depended on 'power' of tackle. Why was this wrong? The con-

cept of power in a rod was equated with the muscular strength required to bring out the action of the rod.

Yet, if you analyse it properly, you soon realise that distance casting depends on altogether different factors. It depends on two things – line speed in the air and a 'narrow loop' on the back cast. The hefty and slow rods failed because they gave neither of these things except, perhaps, by prodigious effort. At this stage let me branch off at a tangent in asking the question: 'Why did still-water casting develop on wrong lines at that time?'

Of course there were men in Britain who knew the secrets of distance casting, and these were the tournament casters. As bad luck would have it, tournament casting was moving away from ordinary fishing in its endeavour to establish itself as a sport recognised in its own right. There was precious little dialogue between fishing and competition and, indeed, the tournament men have often said that their events were poor spectacles for the general public. So the practical casting was developed by those who had no competitive experience, and history has shown this to be a very bad thing. The trade followed the flag, rod-making firms turning out the slow-actioned ten-footers, and this pattern remained unchanged until the late sixties.

I now describe my own part in changing the pat-

Here's to the next time!

EVERY trout you hook will give a tremendous fight – just like this fish is doing to Geoffrey Bucknall on a lake near Sevenoaks in Kent. But keep a tight line on the fish and play it right to the landing net. And it will be yours! But do take care when unhooking a trout – especially if, like Geoff, you wish to return it to the lake. To grow bigger and give another fight!

tern, or rather the part played by a duodenal ulcer which gave me anguished protests at the strain applied on my system by the so-called reservoir rods of that era. 'Surely there must be a way in which casting technique can replace this tread-mill?' I groaned after a session at Blagdon with the long brute of a rod. And I began to think about it, to discuss it with friends and to try out an entirely new system at an evening institute in Peckham. This new system was the 'light shooting head'.

I started with a simple assumption that if distance casting depended on line speed in the air, then how could I manage to achieve it within a light tackle system? But first, why is line speed necessary?

The average caster can only keep aloft a certain length of line. For the sake of argument, I'll put it at 12yds. To reach 20yds, therefore, he has either to sweep a very long line backwards and forwards, which is difficult, or he has to 'shoot' the remaining eight yards at the climax of the cast.

To shoot maximum line you need maximum velocity in the air to pull it out through the rod rings. You see, immediately you begin to think it out, you are in a different ball game because line speed has nothing to do with the length of the rod, nor its weight and power in the old sense.

Part of it is derived from the rod's action. If the rod is relatively stiff with a fast tip action, then its line must move more rapidly through the air. If, as you cast, you can pull the line through the rings with your left hand (assuming you are a right-handed caster) then you add to the line speed. And if you can also reduce the friction of the line moving through the rod rings, then you're beginning to think in terms of ultimate performance.

A stiffish rod with a fast tip action doesn't need to be particularly long, a fact tournament experience could have passed over to us since before the last war. We settled on the Hardy 'Triumph' rod in those days before hollow glass, because it seemed as if this rod had grown out of competitive casting. It could easily drive a lightish shooting head of manageable lengths to distances beyond the reach of the ten-foot cucumbers then in vogue. Moreover it would do this with a minimum of effort, say only two or three double-haul routines to build up the blast-off speed for the final shoot.

To cut a long story short, the new philosophy was first described in my book *Fly Fishing Tactics on Still Water*, first published in 1968. I expected some contention, but the furore surpassed even my worst fears simply because an established system was to be overturned. It was to take some time yet, but the supreme irony is that some of those who attacked the new system as being of no value today tell me that I never developed the idea at all. The record, though, speaks for itself. .

Today's rods are entirely different. They are lighter, faster and shorter. I doubt we still have the best casting tool, not through lack of knowledge, for at any rate we are on the right track now. The inhibition is merely due to the lack of casting expertise, especially in Southern England. This is probably due again to the lack of influence of tournament casting, for if that enthusiasm had spilled over into angling, then a network of competent instruction would have sprung up.

We should have had regional casting associations, or even had them in our big cities, as in America or Scandinavia. Instead, anglers frequently progressed by trial and error, and because you can eventually cast some sort of a line by sheer persistence, they settled for that, perhaps even believing that their tiring routine was true casting.

I have met many anglers who cast a reasonable line without ever knowing what a flexing fly rod feels like, because their muscles are providing the power that the misused rod cannot generate. The

The blood knot is used for tying two pieces of nylon and in making up casts. A 'third hand' is an advantage. Two pieces of hardboard are shaped as shown and then nailed together. The line is clamped between the hardboard. A lollipop stick is then pushed between the strands of nylon and given three turns before the ends of the line are pulled tight.

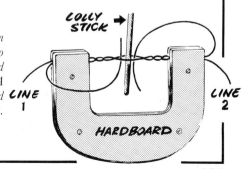

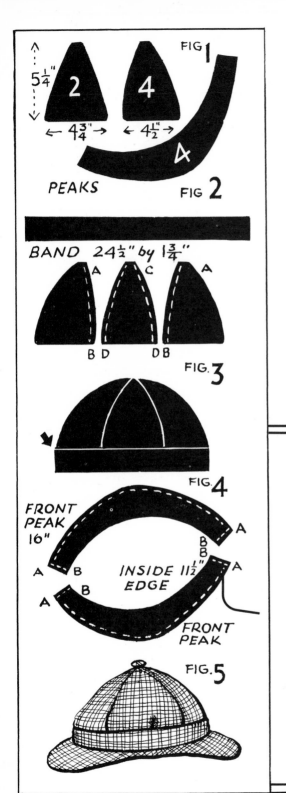

FIG 1

5¼"

← 4¾" →   ← 4½" →

PEAKS

FIG 2

BAND 24½" by 1¾"

A   C   A

B D   D B

FIG. 3

FIG. 4

FRONT
PEAK
16"

A   B

INSIDE 11½"
EDGE

B
B
A

A
B

A

FRONT
PEAK

FIG. 5

commonly heard heartcry 'I don't need to throw a long line' can well be translated into 'I cannot throw a long line'.

I can throw a long line. My best distances under nice conditions, with say my 'Two Lakes' or 'Powercast' rods and double taper lines, are 31 yards. I've measured these casts, and I've always thought them pretty good until more expert friends have pointed out the errors I grew up with, such as twisting slightly at the trunk, or pulling too early on the back cast, small things like that which remove me from the top flight tournament men. I think I can correct them with constant practice, but I know if those errors had never been explained to me, I would have been satisfied for ever, without realising there were any points to watch. The truth is that you cannot see yourself, least of all with trained eyes.

The fundamental question is this: Do we want to become good casters? Yes, I know we all catch fish within our present limitations, and perfectionism can be neurotic. I think it human nature though to search for best performance, and for bank fishermen, farther out must mean more fish..

To this can be added the sheer joy that comes

If you want to get ahead ... get a deerstalker!

FIGURE 1: Cut two and four panels (six pieces) to the sizes shown and cut out the four peak shapes. Peak sizes are shown in Figure 4.

The band is cut next (Figure 2) and seam AB to CD to make half the crown. Complete the crown by seaming the halves together. Seam the band around the bottom of the crown, as arrowed in Figure 3. Then taking two pieces of peak, seam AB to AB (Figure 4).

Next, seam both peaks around outside edge. Turn through and machine row stitching to reinforce. Seam inside of peak to bottom edge.

Cut the lining to the shape of the crown pieces, but add one inch to the length. Stitch by hand to cover seams. Decorate with a button on top and put a feather in the band (Figure 5).

If at first you don't succeed...

Having cast out a fly on a floating line, Geoffrey Bucknall waits for a fish to take his fly. The waders give him extra casting distance as sometimes the fish are a little way out from the bank. 'But I always try the first casts on dry land,' he says.

from complete mastery, the stage when others confess that you make it all look so easy.

If we now consider the actual flies, we see the same delayed evolution. For years the traditional loch flies sufficed, scaled-up versions of popular river patterns like Butcher or Peter Ross. Then, after the war, nymphs were invented, not so much to imitate natural fauna but to act efficiently at various depths and speeds of retrieve.

In fairly recent times, John Goddard and C. F. Walker have invented series of imitative flies for still water, copying the various sedges and buzzers on which trout feed. The strange thing is that the homework for these patterns was done on smaller commercial fisheries.

We now have new flies added to the traditional range. Some of these are frankly imitative of still-water insect life, such as the buzzer pupae, which copy the pupal form of the non-stinging gnat which hatches in profusion from lakes on summer evenings. Prior to their emergence as adult flies, the pupae lie, feeble and vulnerable to the trout, as they are trapped in the surface film. Development has also taken place in the 'lure', a large, attractive fly designed to provoke the predatory instinct of the fish rather than to deceive it by imitation.

Perhaps the most interesting new lure is the 'Beastie', a curiously long marabou lure with a weighted head, which dives and wiggles in the water like a wounded small fish. This lure, in its black/orange or white/pink versions, killed fish in large numbers on waters like Grafham and Hanningfield this past season.

Both of these types of fly, the close imitation or the provocative lure, are based on a simplified understanding of the feeding behaviour of the trout. This fish can wander untempted over inert fauna in the cold water of early spring, for its appetite is triggered only by the activity of its prey. At this time, move something bright across the trout's vision, and it will lunge in fury. Later, when the sun warms up the margins of the lake and insect life bursts into activity, the fish may be programmed into feeding only on one size, colour and form of food at a given time and this is when the imitative approach is vital. Both types of feeding response can be exploited, but the trick is knowing by experience how and when to make a tactical choice.

This, then, is reservoir trouting in all its glory, at once both frustrating and rewarding. It is one of those rare sports which marries physical and intellectual skills, and such sports are the most challenging. To the average angler, mastery seems always just beyond attainment, like the Holy Grail shining on the horizon. Yet, every dog has his day and the time comes when in the midst of reverie, one wakes up to the monstrous rainbow catapulting out of the water as the line sings from the reel. This memory keeps me patient during those long, fruitless periods of automatic casting, sometimes when the sun beats down on a brassy lake and the head feels fit to burst open.

I know the evening is coming, with all of the promise of great fish sipping down buzzers or plucking sedges from the surface. And so I stay with that lunatic obsession to reach the unreachable, that extra yard to drop my fly in that ever-widening ripple, which may bring the icy water over the tops of my waders.

It's a wonderful life.

TEACH-IN ON FLAT FISH

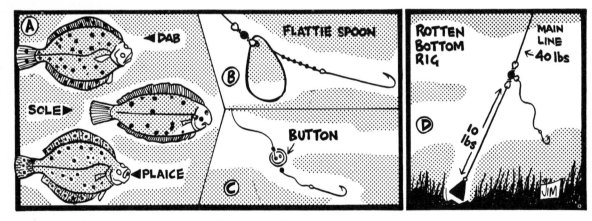

ALL flat fish (Picture A) are good to eat. Dabs are caught in enormous numbers from piers and steeply-sloped beaches. The average weight is half a pound.

The sole is elongated in shape and can grow to 4lb. It is not really an inshore species and so is mostly caught by the angler who uses a boat.

Plaice are not active fish and they stay close inshore. Although the rod-caught record stands at 7lb 15oz, fish of one to two pounds are more frequent. A plaice has distinctive red spots.

To catch a flat fish, just move a baited spoon (Picture B) slowly across the seabed. If a button (Picture C) is fitted to the cast, it will disturb the sand and attract the fish.

When fishing over rocky ground, use a Rotten Bottom (Picture D). If the line does get fast, it will then break off at the weakest point, which is near the sinker – and save loss of line and hooks.

TEACH-IN on natural baits

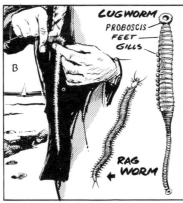

LUGWORM
PROBOSCIS
FEET
GILLS

RAG WORM

CASTS

RUBBY DUBBY BAG.

GORDON.

ALL FISH have a lateral line of sensitive nerves which react to sound waves and vibration. The movement of small fish, crabs and even worms, are transmitted to the predator. The size, speed of movement, and location of the prey reach the hunter as if from a computer.

Fish can also see, smell and taste food. They are not always selective feeders, and when hungry they take any bait offered – in case the other fish gets there first. Feeding fish cannot afford to relax if they want to grow fat. Fresh natural baits are better than preserved ones.

Drawing A: Orderly trenching is the best method of digging the ragworm which abound in muddy estuaries. They come from sandy beaches and betray their presence by 'casts'.

Drawing B: The worms are fed to the hook via the orifice in the head.

Drawing C: Rubby-dubby is easily made from crushed crab, fish-heads, offal and liver. Packed into a muslin bag and trailed from the rear of a boat, the underwater 'cloud' of food will attract fish to the bulk offerings on rod and line.

TEACH-IN on fishing at sea

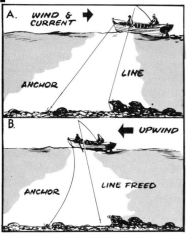

A. WIND & CURRENT

ANCHOR

LINE

B.

UPWIND

ANCHOR

LINE FREED

C. PUMPING IN

GORDON

TOO MANY good boatmen still know too little about fishing. They are mainly interested in getting the angler safely to a good mark, and back again. When at anchor (A), wind and currents make it impossible to free the line when it snags. An experienced boatman will put his craft 'into reverse' (B) and save your tackle.

It is important for the angler to keep as near to the hooked fish as possible. Keeping a tight line by a continuous and unhurried pumping action (C) keeps contact with the fish, and at the same time allows the angler to recover line. Reel in when the rod is at the bottom of the downward stroke.

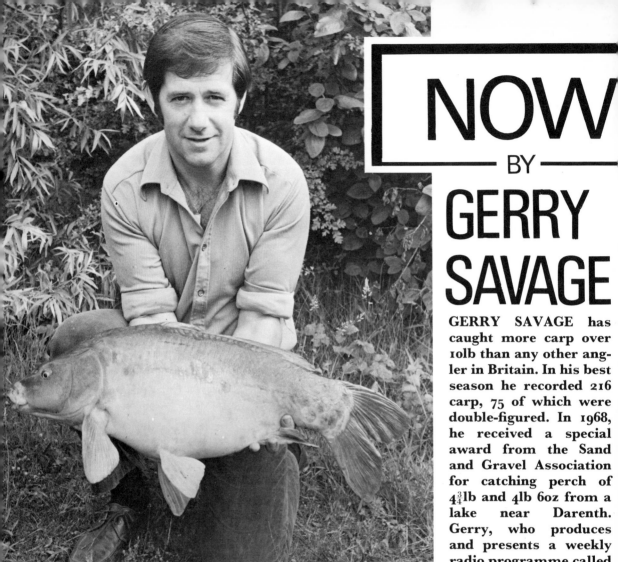

NOW
BY
GERRY SAVAGE

GERRY SAVAGE has caught more carp over 10lb than any other angler in Britain. In his best season he recorded 216 carp, 75 of which were double-figured. In 1968, he received a special award from the Sand and Gravel Association for catching perch of 4¾lb and 4lb 6oz from a lake near Darenth. Gerry, who produces and presents a weekly radio programme called 'Good Fishing', is married and lives with his wife Gill and three children in Kent.

Gerry Savage and a splendid 15lb mirror carp, which fell to catfood paste. He once caught a 26½lb mirror carp on 6lb line from a public water near Dartford, Kent.

F OR thrills, excitement and nerve-tingling tension there's nothing to equal fishing for carp. The sight of line racing from the spool, the split-second that seems an eternity before striking, and the answering battle curve of the rod are all guaranteed to set the pulse racing and the adrenalin working overtime.

I've been a carp lover since I was a teenager but I took up the serious pursuit of carp in 1962. Then,

the waters that held big fish were relatively few but now, thanks to a stocking policy adopted by most of the river authorities, carp are present in large numbers in most of our waters, particularly in the Midlands and the South, where 20lb fish are fairly common.

Forget the myth that carp are impossible fish to tempt. They're not the easiest of fish and won't oblige by jumping on the end of the hook at the

CATCH A CARP!

drop of a bait. But, with the right tackle and careful preparation, they can be caught and fairly regularly.

First the tackle. I use a $10\frac{1}{2}$ft fast taper rod to my own design. But there are several excellent carp rods on the market and they all basically do the same job, though some prefer the 11ft version for long-range casting. A fixed spool reel is the optimum for the carp angler. It incorporates easy casting with trouble-free action and my reel is a high-speed retrieve model which, as the name suggests, enables me to pick up line very quickly, an aid that can prove very valuable.

As to lines, I usually stick to 8lb breaking strain, though on clear and snag-free waters I often scale down to sometimes as little as 4lb b.s. For snaggy and weedy swims, I increase the strain to as much as 17lb.

Now the very important question of water craft. There are carp hot-spots in every lake and there are areas that are totally unproductive, so knowledge of these is essential.

First of all, look for islands. They are a good pointer to gravel and sand bars and some of my best catches have come from these landmarks. Next in line are reeds, weed beds and other shallow areas. To find the last-named, you'll need a plummet and a few hours invested in a fact-finding walk around the lakeside before deciding where to fish could yield a healthy profit.

Next the question of baits, and never before has the carp angler had such a variety to choose from. A few years ago, when I wrote a series of articles on 'special' baits for carp for a national angling newspaper, eyebrows were raised when I advised anglers to try tinned cat and dog food. One angry correspondent even put pen to paper to suggest that, by following my instructions, carp anglers would encourage pollution. This doesn't happen, of course. And now tinned and packet pet food has become something of a standard bait for carp fishers. Here's how you prepare it.

Take one 8oz tin or similar of finely minced cat or dog food – the lumpy variety is alright but it requires mixing thoroughly or mincing – then add 1oz of flour and sufficient breadcrumbs to obtain a firm paste before rolling into balls approximately $\frac{3}{4}$–1oz each.

These can be taken to the lake in a wide-mouthed vacuum flask to preserve hardness. But if you'd like to use a softish bait to tempt the carp, here's a useful dodge. Place the soft paste balls in a freezer overnight, then the following morning use that flask. This will keep the balls hard, they won't come off the hook irrespective of the force used when casting, and minutes after hitting the water the bait will have thawed, presenting an inviting offering to any feeding carp.

To thread the line through a frozen bait, use a baiting needle and then tie the hook on afterwards. If you prefer to use soft baits without freezing, use a crust-retaining pad under the bend of the hook and a small piece of Biro-type tube which is inserted into the top of the bait to avoid line splitting.

The basic concoctions I've mentioned can be made even more exotic by adding things like gravy

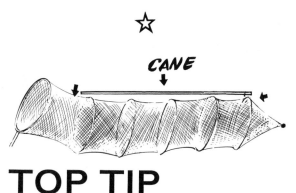

CANE

TOP TIP

Keep nets do not always fully extend in shallower water. To give the fish more room in the net, insert a cane. The cane is cut slightly longer than the measurement from the second ring to the bottom ring of the net.

stock and flavouring. But never forget the simple but successful well-tried baits like bread crust, flake and worms which in the long run, will account for just as many carp as the 'specials'. Even so, variety is the spice of life and I've had days when my bait box has contained an infinite variety of baits yet only one has been acceptable. And, of course, the following session it's been quite the reverse. They're fussy creatures, carp!

Carp fishing is so popular nowadays that the increased pressure on our waters leads to a bait 'going off' very quickly. Anything new will be snapped up almost immediately by feeding carp, fully versed in what baits are a must to avoid. And this is when those subtle differences can pay off, besides of course that watercraft and careful preparation I mentioned earlier.

My colleague John Probert and I once had a bonanza catch of carp topped by a 26½lb mirror. All these fish fell to sausage bait when we'd previously been advised that potato was the only bait to use for that particular water. So it does pay to improvise. One final point: because of the present-day popularity of carp fishing it's not necessary to ground bait heavily.

Follow my instructions, add one or two of your own ideas and I'm prepared to guarantee you'll catch carp.

=== ☆ ===

TEACH-IN on fishing from HIGH PLACES

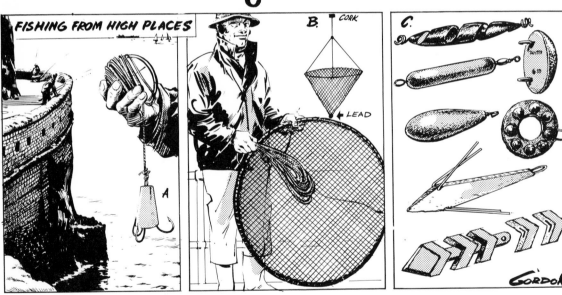

FISH will hang on to the water to the last possible moment. Spreading the tail and side-fins as they are winched up puts tremendous pressure on the rod. The resistance is so great that often the hook-hold tears free.

Sizeable fish can be lifted only with a drop-gaff (A) or a drop-net (B). Three large cod hooks, linked together and set into a lead mould, will lift the heaviest of fish if the cord is stout.

To make a drop-net use a bicycle wheel rim or an iron hoop. Paint it well or cover it with a plastic coat to prevent corrosion. Attach the harness as shown. Then wire in a small weight at the base of the net.

The sinkers (illustrated in C) have specific uses. The spiral is wound to the line well above the bait. The swivel on the barrel lead prevents line-twist. The pear-shaped weight is for long casting and a rolling leger. The flat and coffin leads are for grip and anchorage. The bottom weight is adjustable to tide and current.

Teach-In on pier fishing

LOOK DOWN from a pier when the tide is low and you will see a maze of wood and iron supports which are hidden when the tide rises. These supports are covered with barnacles and seaweed which attract fish, but pick a reasonably clear area to drop your baited hook.

Hooks come in many shapes and sizes (Picture 2). It is false economy to use old and rusted hooks. Always examine the point and the barb to make sure they are intact and sharp.

A foraging fish is not too choosy about what it will eat (Picture 3). Mackerel, bass and flat fish hang around piers and they will take a moving lure such as a spinner and a baited spoon.

117

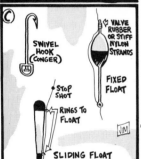

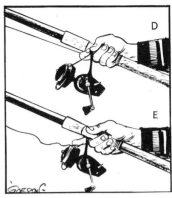

TEACH-IN...

on casting with a fixed spool

NYLON is full of bounce. Loose coils flying off the spool do not improve the angler's temper. But tangles are easy to avoid if the spool is correctly loaded. The secret is to have the coils just below the shaped lip, as in C (A is overloaded, and B has too little). It's as easy to cast with a fixed spool reel as it is to breathe. Note the correct position of the reel and the appropriate grip (D). The pick-up bale arm is brought over, and the line is clipped tight between the rod and the index finger. As the cast is made (E), the forefinger releases the line, which automatically peels from the spool.

Keep an eye on the shore line if you're fishing the drift

A GOOD boatman always knows where to find fish and, by taking a mark through the shore line (A), he can pinpoint the exact spot to drop anchor. Sometimes shoals of fish move around with the currents and they follow the food lanes as the tide ebbs and flows. It is then that the angler lifts the anchor and 'fishes the drift'.

The boat moves surprisingly fast and the angler must be always on the alert because hooks and lines snag on the uneven sea bed (B). To avoid losing tackle, the reel and the length of line should be constantly adjusted.

Use the correct hooks and floats (C). Conger hooks are swivelled; cod hooks have a very large gape. And flattie hooks have a small, round bend to a longish shank.

A sliding float is for fishing at varying depths; the fixed float is for use when the boat is at anchor. Floats are used to indicate a bite, but in sea fishing they also serve to keep the tempting bait just clear of the marauding crabs on the sea bed.

TOP TIP

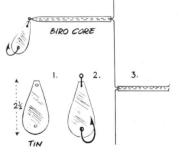

To catch a cod, cut a few discs from tin, pass the hooks through, and use biro tubes to make a paternoster lure.

Teach-In on mackerel

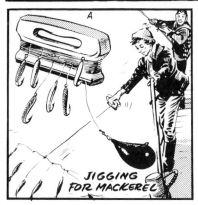

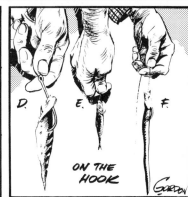

MACKEREL give themselves up in large numbers during summertime. Boat anglers after shark must first of all catch mackerel for bait. The hand-held Jigger (A) is new from Norway. A loop insert in the weight allows 12 baits to fish at the same time. Pier anglers with light trout rods have good sport by whipping the lure through the shoal when it swims close.

A filleted slice of mackerel (B) or tapered strips of fresh herring are good baits for tope and skate. The hook is placed in the broadest part (C). A hook baited-up for tope is shown in D, and E depicts a preserved sprat on the hook to catch a bass. A sand-eel on terminal tackle for large conger, coalfish and bass is shown in F.

Sea fish follow the tides in and out. They feed with the flow. The slackest period for taking fish is when the tide is at peak high and peak low.

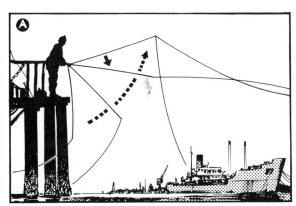
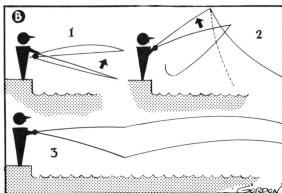

UNDERHAND CASTING

SHIPS' hawsers, bystanders and pier stanchions sometimes put the beginner off fishing altogether, because he cannot get his bait clear of the obstacles. In Picture A, all the casting is under and forward. Repeating the pendulum swing below the pier and lifting the rod-tip higher each time, the line and weight is released to shoot forward.

In Picture B, where the angler does not have the advantage of a high platform, successful fishing is achieved by: (1) Pointing the rod in the right direction and holding the bait tight as a spring. (2) Lift the rod smartly and let the bait swing free. Quickly lower the rod top as the bait shoots out. (3) Follow through and forward, until the bait hits the water.

119

AFRICAN

by John Goddard

JOHN GODDARD is one of Britain's top trout fishermen and author of several books on the subject. He has been fishing for 40 years, but in the past few years he has also specialised in deep-sea or big-game fishing, mainly abroad. He is vice-chairman of the British Association of Tacklemakers, and was until recently Chairman of the Angling Foundation from its inception.

IN a last desperate effort to regain its freedom the mighty fish gave a lunge with its tail, sending a cascade of water over the side of the boat and soaking us both to the skin; next second the gaff dug in and the still struggling fish was hauled in over the side of the boat where it lay thumping the deck with its tail. Looking down at the dying perch we estimated its weight at well over 50lb. We solemnly shook hands, as this was no ordinary perch but our first Nile perch for which we had travelled over 6,000 miles.

At the time Leslie Moncrieff and I were on a fishing tour of Kenya in East Africa and our first expedition in this country was a three-day visit to Lake Rudolph in Northern Kenya to endeavour to catch the mighty Nile perch and also tiger fish. Rudolph is a vast sheet of water, over 170 miles long

by 30 miles wide, and is situated in one of the most isolated areas in Africa. In fact it was only mapped in 1924 on an expedition led by Vivian Fuchs, the well-known explorer.

Apart from the two fishing camps on the western shores of the lake the only other inhabitants of this area are the Turkana, one of the most primitive tribes in Africa, who eke out a precarious existence living mainly on fish from the lake. The eastern shores of the lake are completely uninhabited, consequently wild game is abundant and it is a fascinating experience to fish from a boat close in along this shore. One can observe lion, zebra, giraffe and many other species that come down to the water's edge to quench their thirst.

From Nairobi it is possible to reach the lake by Landrover, but as there are no roads this is nearly all

ADVENTURE
... in search of the mighty Nile PERCH and the fearsome-looking TIGER FISH

cross-country work and takes two or three days. We therefore travelled in comfort in a small Piper plane and were fortunate to have an experienced bush pilot, who showed us many places of interest en route, including a small lake that is rarely visited.

One shore appeared to be a peculiar reddish pink in colour and it was not until the pilot brought the plane down low over the water that we saw thousands of pink flamingoes standing rank upon rank in the shallow water. Further on we flew low over another lake on which we observed several herds of hippos, and lying along the muddy shores were many crocodiles. In the centre of this lake was a small island which we slowly circled while the pilot pointed out many very large birds that were in residence. These he explained were Goliath herons, among the rarest birds in the world and found only in this area.

The most effective way of catching Nile perch is undoubtedly by trolling large lures or plugs from a boat. Boats are normally available at the camp; unfortunately we found that most of the better ones were temporarily out of action due to mechanical trouble. Fortunately Bob McConnel, the local fisheries officer for Rudolph, came to our rescue with the fisheries launch.

Bob is a grand fellow and for the last ten years has lived in splendid isolation on the shores of the lake. He has an intimate knowledge of the fish, and largely due to him we had one marvellous day when

we caught more than 400lb of these fish, the two best specimens weighing 84lb and 73lb.

Leslie and I had brought our beachcasting rods and reels, as we were particularly keen to try and catch some of these Nile perch from the shore. The first morning after our arrival saw us out on the shore near the camp just as dawn was breaking. Using 4oz leads and a fillet of fish on a single hook, we had no difficulty in casting out well over the 100 yards. This seemed to impress the natives; on the other hand they were equally unimpressed at our failure to catch anything, for despite many bites we failed to make contact.

Later that day we were discussing our lack of success with Robin Bewg, manager of the camp, and he assured us that the fish were probably feeling the resistance of the lead after they picked the bait

John Goddard holds up two average-sized tiger fish for examination by his young Turkana assistants.

up. He then went on to explain that many of the local Turkana children fished in the vicinity of the camp casting out from the shore with handlines. Their tackle was crude but effective – a length of strong nylon fastened to a large treble hook. While we were quite prepared to bow to local knowledge, we were more than a little puzzled as to how we could adapt their methods to our gear, as it is quite impossible to cast a piece of bait with no lead from a multiplying reel.

However, we need not have worried as next morning we were each supplied with two diminutive native children to teach us how to fish. This proved to be a most illuminating experience, as these youngsters certainly knew what they were about.

First of all they showed us how to bait up; a strip of fish was cut and hung from each point of the treble so that it resembled a skirt. Next they stripped about 60 yards of line from the reel and coiled it at their feet, and then one of them picked up the monofilament holding it about a yard from the baited hook. He whirled it round and round his head faster and faster, released it at the psychological moment and it went out straight as a die for well over 50 yards. To say we were astounded would be putting it mildly!

This method was certainly effective, as we found the fish would pick up the bait and move off quite confidently with it. After they had taken about 20 yards of line we would hit them hard. Fishing that morning from the local hot-spot we caught several different species of fish, but alas none of the larger perch which we were really after. The next morning, which was to be our last, we were beaten to our hot-spot by two Americans who were staying at the

THEY WENT 6,000 MILES FOR THIS

Bob McConnel gaffs another splendid Nile perch for author Goddard.

camp. As a result we were to witness a most amusing incident.

The boys were baiting up and throwing out for them as they had done for us, and they were using cheap glass Japanese rods and fixed spool reels that they had borrowed from the camp. Neither of them had done much fishing before and did not realise the clutches on the reels were jammed solid. They had been fishing for over two hours without a bite when suddenly one of them gave a shout. We could see his rod bent almost double and he was obviously into a good fish. Slowly but surely he was being dragged towards the water's edge, when his colleague shouted: 'Don't forget the crocodiles!'

I will swear he went white through his suntan as he called desperately for assistance. Much to our surprise the line did not break with two of them

heaving on the rod, and in due course a Nile perch weighing nearly 50lb was hauled up the beach.

Even now I can still visualise the excitement of the moment, as neither of them had ever seen a fish of such proportions before, let alone caught one. He then insisted upon his friend photographing him with his catch, as spluttering with excitement and dripping with sweat he endeavoured to hold up the fish which was almost as big as he was. He said: 'You gotta get a good photo of this as my old Mamma at home will never believe me ... You sure you gotta film in the camera? ... You certain the damn thing's in focus?' and so on and so on.

Apart from the perch, Rudolph holds several other varieties of fish including the fearsome-looking tiger fish. They have the most formidable mouth of teeth of any fish in the world, and even a small specimen can take a finger off with one snap of its

...AND IT WAS WORTH EVERY INCH!

Coming aboard is 50lb of fighting Nile perch, complete with bait.

jaws. They are a fascinating species to angle for – terrific fighters but extremely difficult to hook as their mouths are all bone. In this lake they do not go very large, the average size being about 2lb, but we had great sport with them from the shore using light spinning outfits and small silver lures.

They tend to move along the shore in shoals chasing the fry on the surface, and I am convinced that the most effective method of catching them would have been on a fly rod. Unfortunately I did not have one with me and there was none available in the camp.

On our return from the heat and desolation of Rudolph, we had a couple of days on lovely Lake Naivasha in the cool of the Kenya highlands. This is a small lake compared with Rudolph, though by our standards it is still very large. A very picturesque water, the tree-lined shores are full of exotic birds, and floating islands of papyrus dot large sections of the lake. These are often fringed by extensive beds of water lilies frequented by storks, herons and other wading birds, while on the open water pelicans are often observed.

This lake is famous for its black bass fishing and very good it is, too. Catches of 20 to 30 fish in a day are not uncommon, and several fish over 7lb are taken every season.

One corner of the lake is full of dead trees standing in the water, and was so typical of the pictures beloved by American bass fishermen I mentally labelled it 'Lunkers Corner'. The fishing here is all

What a way to end a holiday!

IT'S the end of an exhilarating three-day expedition to darkest Africa, and no wonder there are smiles on the faces of our intrepid explorers! In the above picture, they are examining part of their final day's catch – and those two Nile perch weighed in at 84lb and 73lb. Their bag also included the adult tiger fish on the right. Says Goddard: 'They have the most formidable mouth of teeth of any fish in the world.' Yes, one to avoid!

done from boats and we were fortunate to have as our guide Derek Campbell, a first-class angler and an expert on the bass of Naivasha.

This type of fishing was foreign country to my colleague Leslie, so after catching one or two small bass he decided to concentrate on the photography. We were fishing with popping plugs for the larger bass and Les was particularly keen to obtain a photograph of a big bass. He is very placid by nature and rarely gets annoyed, but on this occasion he got so mad he threatened to throw the camera in the water as we lost bass after bass in the heavy weed. Three times we actually had fish between 4–6lb almost ready for the net, but still they threw the hook at the last moment.

Sad to relate, we never did manage to boat any of the better fish, probably due to the fact we were using extremely light tackle – undoubtedly a mistake with the heavy weed in the area we were fishing.

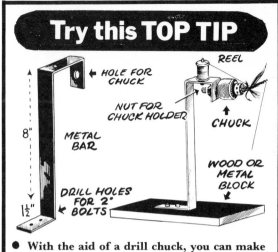

Try this TOP TIP

● **With the aid of a drill chuck, you can make this fly-tying vice.**

Get it right at the seaside

BEACH CASTING

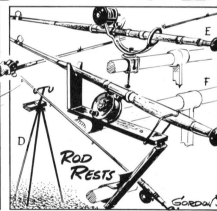

ROD RESTS

GORDON

MOST of today's sea-rods are made of fibreglass, either hollow or solid. They are impervious to salt water, powerful and strong, stand up to very hard punishment and will not warp. Heavy weights that carry the long, heavy-loaded line demand plenty of 'give' from the heaving rod.

Some sea fish feed close in where the breakers churn up the sand and disturb seaweed. But it's an advantage to get well out into the gulleys and passageways between the rocks. These drawings give the basic rules for comfortable long beach-casting.

The stance and grip in Figure A is the correct starting

position. B is wrong, because the feet are too close together and the rod angled too far down. C shows the manual operation of braking multiplier-level wind reels. Over-runs are avoided if the line is stopped immediately after hitting the water.

On a windy pier, all rods need to be firmly established, otherwise damage is done to the reel and the rod whippings. A few hours at home assembling the anchorage patterns illustrated (D, E and F) will mean that the untidy tying rags, so often used as stop-gap, can be scrapped.

TEN TOP KNOTS

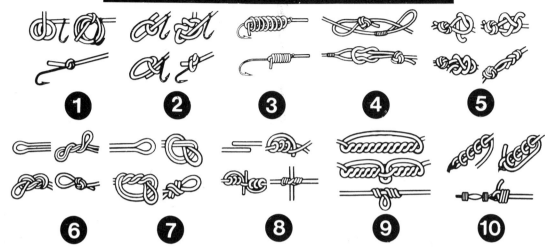

1   **2**   **3**   **4**   **5**

6   **7**   **8**   **9**   **10**

HERE are ten top knots that every angler should know. Each simple stage for tying the knots is shown on the diagram. Always finish off by pulling the nylon very tightly. Here is what the knots are used for:

1, Two-Circle Turle; 2, Two-Turn Turle; 3, Domhof – for attaching the cast to the hook.

4, Two Loops; 5, Tucked Sheet Bend – for attaching the cast to the line.

6, Blood Bight; 7, Double Overhand Loop – for making a safe loop in nylon line.

8, Double Three-fold Blood; 9, Blood Loop Dropper – for attaching a dropper length of nylon to take on extra fly.

10, Four-Turn Half Blood – for attaching the swivel.

TEACH-IN on the right names

EXPERT fishermen are often unable to put the right name to the fish they catch (Picture A). A small chub and a large dace are very much alike, but a closer look at the edge of the fins will show the difference.

Roach and rudd can also cause confusion, but if a line is drawn from the back fin to the belly of each fish, the positioning of the underbelly (anal) fin is clearly different.

Conger eels (Picture B) are salt-water fish which can grow to over 100lb. The common eel is a river fish, but after about ten years in the river it migrates to the deeps of the Sargasso Sea to spawn. Note the position of the back fins.

To catch a shark, the line should be at least 200lb breaking strain, and the reel should be big enough to take 350 yards of line. All of the shark family have peculiar tail shapes (Picture C).

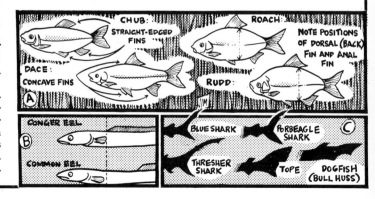

CHUB: STRAIGHT-EDGED FINS

ROACH

NOTE POSITIONS OF DORSAL (BACK) FIN AND ANAL FIN

DACE: CONCAVE FINS

RUDD

A

CONGER EEL

COMMON EEL

B

BLUE SHARK   PORBEAGLE SHARK

THRESHER SHARK   TOPE   DOGFISH (BULL HUSS)

C

A message of cheer for those by the reservoir

by LEONARD PARKIN

LEONARD PARKIN, the ITN news-caster and foreign correspondent, has been fishing since he was a child in Yorkshire. He doesn't really mind what he fishes for, although these days he prefers fly fishing for trout with his own rudimentary attempts at flies. In a working life which has included wars, the Congo, Algeria, the Middle East, he has also spent a long time in America. At home he has tried to restore and manage a mile of a once famous trout stream and he is a dedicated conservationist.

FOR the still-water trout fisherman, the heaving, featureless acres of one of our big water supply reservoirs often induce feelings of defeat even before the first cast has been made. The problem is that all too often there are no points of reference, no readily recognisable signs to suggest areas where fish may be found; where the experienced fisherman can use his knowledge and the inexperienced employ the charitable advice of other anglers who know the water well.

For most casual visitors to a big reservoir, bank fishing is a voyage of discovery on an inland sea which all too frequently gets nowhere. They tend to find an unoccupied spot, churn muddily through the shallows until they can wade no further, and then spend the day trying to cast a fly out of sight in the hope that one of the tens of thousands of rainbows and browns with which the water is stocked will accept it gratefully. Generally speaking the fish decline the offering, and at the end of the day the fisherman moodily fills in a nil return on his permit and curses the law of averages which has come between him and a trout or two.

I would be very surprised if there are not a great many trout fishermen who visit British still waters who cannot recognise themselves in that rather discouraging sketch. So let's see what we can do to cheer them up and offer, if not exactly advice, a few observations to make them feel better.

The scene at the end of the fishing day is typical. After ten hours or so of flogging away with Peter Ross, Mallard and Claret, Greenwell's Glory, Teal and Green, Wickham's Fancy, Iven's Green and Brown Whatsit, Walker's Chomping Polystickle, So and So's Deer-hair bodied Missionary Variant with the neon magenta tag and hot-orange hackle, Someone Else's Muddled Matuka, the double-hooked Bloody Butcher and anything else for that matter which happened to catch the eye in the fly box, the magic moment arrives.

The lambswool patch on the lapel of the fishing jacket is festooned with a limp and sodden collection of failed flies and lures; the spools of nylon are a day shorter after their succession of rescues on wind knots and birds' nests; the wrist and shoulders are aching with the exertion of long-casting and double-hauling; the coffee flask is empty, the sausage rolls finished; there's an ominous damp feeling in the foot of the right wader; the eyes are aching with peering into the distance through polarising lenses; and there is a mounting sense of frustration as the pale sun goes down and the breeze drops to 'light airs'.

This trout was caught at Weir Wood reservoir in Sussex – a day-ticket fishery that is annually stocked with brown and rainbow trout by the Southern Water Authority.

But in spite of all that, in spite of having caught nothing on a perfect day for fishing, the thought of the magic moment quickens the imagination. The evening rise is about to begin. There may still be time to catch a limit. The cast is greased down to the last half inch; the tiny buzzers are tied on. Up into the backcast, once forward, back again and then off into the surface film they go to await the delicious inevitable, the boiling rises of avidly-feeding trout.

What optimists we are! Alas, the inevitable evening rise turns out not to be inevitable at all; in fact, people will tell you they haven't seen a real evening rise since 1967! Suddenly, after those agonising minutes of slowly twitching in the nymphs and the final efforts of concentration, darkness falls, and the sense of failure mingles with the sense of outrage at having made an expensive journey to buy an expensive day permit on a so-called prolific water without having seen a fish all day. And it is happening so often lately that the wife is beginning to wonder if you really go fishing at all.

As you reach the fishing hut after the long trudge through the darkness, the welcoming light is on and there is happy chatter around the weighing scales.

Jovial, red-faced men, smiling under their deer-stalkers, flat caps and woolly hats with coloured bobbles on them, are singing tunes of glory as they weigh in their numerous fish.

As you stand there, looking on enviously from the edge of the circle as yet another big rainbow is flopped on to the measuring board, the conversation is always the same. Take heart, for the moral of the story is about to be unfolded.

'What,' you ask timidly, 'did you take that on?'

Mr Successful looks at you patronisingly. 'Oh, just a little yellow-bodied thing, size 18, which I knocked up at home out of a bit of old duster, and a bit of pink hackle from an old hat of my mother-in-law's.'

'Oh well,' you say politely, 'that's about the one combination of colours I didn't try all day.'

Inwardly, you are thinking: 'Like Hell!' And you would be right. It may be that, like many fishermen, this one is simply incapable of giving a straight, truthful answer to a straight question. Or, more probably, there could be more to it than that. If you talk to the bailiffs who manage those enormous reservoirs, and to some of the keen season-ticket men who spend hundreds of hours fishing

WHY ANGLERS MUST PAY TWICE OVER

FISHING is anything but free. Indeed, anglers usually have to pay twice over. Before they can legally wet a line in inland waters, a licence and a permit must be obtained (A).

The licence fee is paid to the Government and it can cost anything from 25p to £15 a season, depending on the type of fish the angler is after. Coarse fishing is cheaper and more plentiful than game fishing.

All fishing rights are owned by somebody. The owners may be a fishing club, town council or a private landlord. They fix the price and the number of permits to be issued – and they also make the rules.

Sea fishing does not require a licence or a permit, but strict size limits for fish are enforced and the little ones must be put back into the sea. So it pays

to carry a ruler or measuring stick (B).

All water bailiffs have the powers of police and are entitled to search the anglers' baskets for illegal

tackle and undersized fish. River keepers and club bailiffs are private employees and have no such powers of search and arrest.

129

there throughout the season, you will discover that there is a good deal of cheating.

A good fly fisherman I know, and whose opinion I respect, said to me on the bank of a Midlands reservoir one day: 'I can tell you this, the most successful guy here hasn't used a fly all season!' He was talking about a fellow who had quickly adopted the conventions of fly fishing. He had bought a deer-stalker to attend his first casting lesson, but the basic principles of fly fishing sportsmanship had so far escaped him.

We all know that there is a good deal of latitude on a fly-only water as to what constitutes a fly and what does not. It seems to boil down to anything artificial which can be cast with a trout rod and fly line. No one I know can cast a half-ounce spinner with a light trout rod, but they are used from boats by people dragging lead-cored lines along the bottom, often in areas where trolling is banned.

Bailiffs find fishermen in action with worms and there are instances of groundbaiting with soaked bread and maggots and then fishing the natural maggot. I suppose if you are allowed to make an artificial maggot out of cream wool to imitate the larva of the drone fly, which trout love, then it is really a nice point as to whether you ought to be allowed to use a real maggot.

However, such things are not allowed; but long acquaintance with reservoirs will convince you that such piffling regulations do not worry some of those who build reputations as mighty catchers of trout. When you know other people are cheating, the temptation to cheat is strong. But in another context, I doubt whether a successful batsman would think much of himself if he used a bat half an inch wider than the regulations allowed.

I doubt whether it matters much whether you catch a trout on a spinner on a lead-cored line in a non-trolling area; it is only yourself you are cheating. I just hope that if you do you will spare me the information, as I inquire timidly from the sidelines as

Here's a sight to gladden the hearts of sad reservoir men – a handsome foursome 'limit' catch of rainbow trout. And so to supper!

you weigh your splendid catch that you caught them in that Force 6 wind on a little old thing made from the fur of your nephew's hamster in its winter coat, fished dry on a 2lb point and cast to cruising fish!

I said take heart. Most of us have to live with the fact that casual visitors to our great stocked reservoirs do not catch many fish. The men who do – and who stay within the rules – are the local experts, season ticket holders who get to know each other well over the years and who form a tight little club of fanatically-keen trout catchers.

They tend to know where at any particular time the fish in the reservoir are to be found, so that unlike the casual visitor they are very rarely fishing dead water. They get to know the way the weather affects their particular reservoir – the effect, for instance, of an on-shore wind blowing for several days. They are never to be found in the easy places to fish, with the wind blowing gently over the left shoulder. You will find them trying to fish nymphs on long leaders into or across the wind on the other side of the reservoir, because they know that no matter how uncomfortable the conditions are for the fisherman, the fish are going to be where the flies are falling.

Most important, you will find them consulting each other on the telephone, telling each other the truth about what the fish are taking, where, at what sort of speed of retrieve, at what depth, in what size and so on. They give each other patterns of successful flies, nymphs and lures.

The result of all this is that they count their season's catches in hundreds. And this is the rub. A water which claims an average, say, of 1·2 trout per rod day has obviously had some fishermen catching

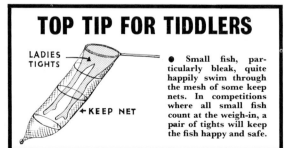

TOP TIP FOR TIDDLERS

LADIES TIGHTS

← KEEP NET

● Small fish, particularly bleak, quite happily swim through the mesh of some keep nets. In competitions where all small fish count at the weigh-in, a pair of tights will keep the fish happy and safe.

more and some less. Those who catch fewer fish subsidise those who catch more.

The casual angler, faced with doubtful methods on the one hand and expert application on the other, is at an obvious disadvantage. And the disadvantage shows when he drives home disconsolately with an empty bag wondering if the reservoir management stocked the place with as many fish as they said they did.

The casual still-water trout fisher is faced with masses of advice from the angling papers. He may take it and decide to use long leaders instead of short, imitation fly life instead of lures, to stalk his fish instead of casting indiscriminately, to forget comfort and go where the fish are, to use a sinking line no matter how difficult and unpleasant it is if that is the only way to make the fly get down to the fish. And he may still catch nothing.

The answer, as with many other activities, is perseverance. And local advice. In my experience it is no use asking the bailiffs or the fishery manager where the fish are likely to be found and what they are taking. Their knowledge tends to be only as good and as recent as the last person who spoke to them, and it might well have been the chap with the little yellow-bodied thing.

'Oh, yes,' they'll say, 'yellow flies seem to be successful just now, a little Invicta perhaps, very small and fished on the surface.' Baloney!

Never be afraid of asking other fishermen on the bank for advice. The close little sect of experts they might belong to is never so secretive as to confuse newcomers intentionally. They try to baffle their friends from time to time, never strangers.

After that, you can forget that some folk around the bank might be lobbing in trout-feed pellets and fishing with either a pellet on one hook of a wee double or a *pelletus vulgaris* fashioned from cork or a tiny ball of deer hair! You can also forget that a great many people know the water better than you ever will.

The thing to do is to try to cast well, think about why you are fishing where you are fishing, experiment with depths and speeds of retrieve and with a limited number of flies, and who knows, perhaps the time will come when you can unfold that bag in which your wife carried away her last nightie from Marks and Sparks, fill it with fish, march off to the weight scales, and tell everyone who asks (and they will) that you picked them up on a little purple affair with a blue jay throat hackle and double split wings, cast to trout you were sure were feeding on corixae.

But if you do not catch anything by now, you will know for certain that the people who count their catches on reservoirs in hundredweights are doing something you are not doing, whatever it is.

Teach-In on the baby salmon

IT IS illegal to take or injure salmon parr. But river fishermen are often ignorant of the differences between a small trout (Picture 1a) and a small salmon (1b). The young fish inhabit the same waters and take the same lures and baits.

A trout is clumsier at the tail, and the mouth is larger than that of the parr. The trout has many more red spots, *while the parr carries eight or ten smokey-blue fingermarks evenly placed along the sides.*

An adult salmon can be safely landed (Picture 2) without the use of gaffs, landing nets or telescopic tailers. When the fish is tired, just grasp it firmly by the 'wrist' of its tail and lift clear of the water. If salmon scales are needed for research, scrape them from the place marked X in Picture 3.

TEACH-IN on beach fishing

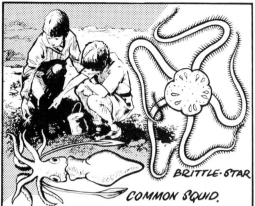

BRITTLE-STAR. COMMON SQUID.

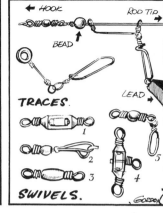

HOOK ROD TIP
BEAD
TRACES. LEAD
SWIVELS.
—GORDON.

AT low tide, rock pools will provide a lot of the bait needed for beach fishing.

Common squid are sometimes washed up dead, but they can be obtained from a fishmonger's deep-freeze. Cut them up into slivers for smaller fish baits. Use them whole when after shark.

Of the starfishes, the brittle star is best for bass. Swivels and end-tackles are made of metal and should be individually tested.

The nylon line and the rod-tip will flex, but the swivel must rigidly stand up to the lunges of a fish.

Some expensive swivels (Figure 3) have a small ball-bearing inserted at each end of the barrel. Others have a useful snap-link (Figures 2 and 5) which is very handy, as it enables the end tackle to be changed without cutting the line to tie a fresh knot.

STERN HOVE TO DRIFT

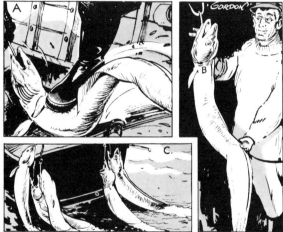

BOAT FISHING

THE best fishing position is at the stern (A). It is almost impossible to land a hooked fish if the boat is drifting over the line and the bait – for then it becomes a keel-hauling operation (C).

Worst possible place for the fisherman to stand is just above the exhaust (B). Breathing in diesel fumes will turn even the best saltwater man a sea-sick green.

EXCITEMENT continues until the very last moment when you're conquering the conger. The fuss reaches a peak when the fish is hauled across the gunwales. But don't rush to unhook the writhing monster too soon. Hold it down with strong boots (A).

Congers easily whip round and bite the hand to the bone. Use pliers to remove the hook. A small conger dwarfs the big-

BEATING A CONGER

gest of men. The muscles just below the head (B) pack a ter-rific force.

Best way to get the catch home is by tying each fish through the mouth with a tow-rope (C).

TEACH-IN
on commercial fishing

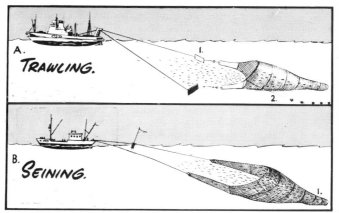

ANGLING is just a sport, strictly speaking, but fishing is done for a living. A single haul of the net by a commercial vessel will scoop out more fish than a dozen rods can take in a lifetime.

A line-caught fish always tastes better than a netted fish because a fish on the hook gets rid of its body wastes before it is landed.

Picture A shows a trawler and net. Water pressure on the 'otter' boards (1) serves to keep the mouth of the net open. A footrope of bobbins (2) rolls across the sea bed to keep apart the gaping mouth of the net.

A seine netter (Picture B) prefers to fish mid-water or near the surface. After making a circular sweep of the net from the first flagged buoy, the long ropes winch it aboard. The pocket (1) is called a 'cod end'.

Plaice are a suitable fish for rearing from eggs. Picture C shows a researcher grading fish and measuring them at the end of a year's growth.

The difference a tide makes . . .

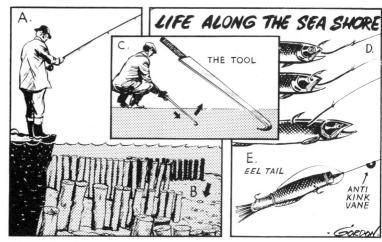

FISHING grounds take on a vastly changed look when the tide is in. Jetty angler (A) did not take the trouble to find out a few things beforehand. Consequently the underwater obstructions lost him a lot of tackle.

By accident, he discovered that successful fishing was only possible when he cast beyond the barriers to the spot marked B.

Sand-eels, a good all-round bait, can be exposed with a garden fork or a hoe. But the tool (C) makes the job less laborious. During the month of August when the moon is shining, sand-eels and whiting are often left swimming in shallow pools on the sand.

Illustrations D show three methods of impaling dead sand-eels for sea fishing. Hundreds of spring salmon fall each season to eel-tail (E) mounted to spinning tackle.

To preserve sand-eels, pack them upright in a clean, screwtop jar filled with a liquid made from formalin (2 parts), glycerine (3 parts) and water (95 parts).

One for you too sister!

*Southend Pier and the mackerel are in!
This youngster watches her big brother
land a couple of fine fish on mackerel
feathers – a useful bait for these fighting species.*

100

YEARS
of
TACKLE

by
Jim
Hardy

DURING the past hundred years, four materials in particular have greatly increased the pleasure and success of the angler. These are bamboo, the finest material from which rods have been made, fibreglass, monofilament and vinyl coating nylon braided core used in the manufacture of fly lines.

Prior to bamboo, lance-wood and greenheart, among many other woods, had been used in the manufacture of rods as we know them. These materials had many disadvantages, perhaps the greatest being that of weight and the fact that they could break easily. Bamboo, carefully hand-planed into sections and glued together, reduced the weight of rods and greatly improved their action over all previously-made rods.

This era started towards the end of the last century. Calcutta cane was used at first, but was discarded for Tonkin bamboo. Tonkin grows in a very small special area in China. It has all the features required to make a good fishing rod and is very much superior to any other type of bamboo. Many attempts have been made to grow Tonkin bamboo in other parts of the world but only that grown in this particular part of China has the correct characteristics.

It was the introduction of bamboo rods, or as they are called today built cane rods, that enabled ladies to take up the gentle art. Before the advent of built cane, rods were generally far too heavy for them; with built cane rods, they could fish with ease and very good anglers they became. In fact, in the 1890s there was a rod on the market called the Princess rod –a copy of one which was specially designed for Her Serene Highness, Princess Victoria of Teck.

Other rods on the market at this time were the Ideal, the Gem and Perfection patterns in special balances suitable for ladies. Ladies' salmon fly rods, cane built, steel centre, with two tops, patent lock

---

JIM HARDY entered the family firm of Hardy Brothers in 1950, after army service in North Africa and Palestine, and an engineering apprenticeship with Vickers Armstrong in Newcastle. He was a competitor for ten successive years in World casting championships, becoming a British, European and World champion in fly and bait casting events.

Jim has fished in America, Canada, Japan, New Zealand, South Africa, Spain, France, Switzerland, Norway and Sweden, as well as throughout the British Isles. He has been responsible for the development of many rods and reels during the past years and has taught casting and fishing in many countries of the world.

joints, bridge rings, universal reel fittings and cork covered handle, 14ft long, were £7 3s 6d.

A perfect rod for ladies' use must of necessity be an easy working one and should not cause any strain either on the arms or back, and in balancing these rods special care had been taken. The rods were sufficiently strong to play heavy fish with a sweet action in the butt, so that they were cast with the least possible exertion.

For an invalid they were also 'peculiarly suitable'. Of course much would depend on the extent of the invalid's disability. An extract from *The Lady* of June 1892 reads: 'The very best for a lady is a split cane of first quality. I have lately seen one greatly more suitable than any I have seen before and this is Hardy's Perfect rod for ladies. They also have reels of special excellence.'

Cane rods manufactured in various ways – non-

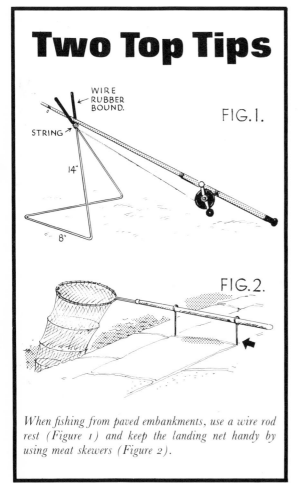

Two Top Tips

WIRE
RUBBER BOUND.

STRING

FIG.1.

14"

8"

FIG.2.

When fishing from paved embankments, use a wire rod rest (Figure 1) and keep the landing net handy by using meat skewers (Figure 2).

agonal, octagonal, hexagonal, pentagonal, hollow built, double built or single built – made up the main armoury of the angler along with greenheart right up to the 1940s. In the late 1940s and early 1950s, another change in rod material arrived, namely fibreglass reinforced plastic or what we usually call fibreglass. This material soon replaced greenheart, but was not a real competitor to built cane for some years.

It took about ten years for fibreglass rods to become perfected. This was due to the fact that fibreglass blanks, from which the rods were made, were manufactured by companies who had no great knowledge or tradition in rod making. Actions, in the early days of fibreglass, were very poor, giving poor casting qualities. In time, improvements were made, particularly when rod makers and fibreglass blank manufacturers eventually got together and produced what we have today, very good fibreglass rods for all branches of angling.

It is interesting to note that although built cane rods went out of favour for a few years, they are still sought keenly by the better fly fishing markets of the world. There is a certain something, difficult to explain, that a good cane fly rod has which a rod from any other material cannot equal. Also, a good cane built rod is a pride of possession.

Recently, carbon reinforced plastic rods (or carbon rods as we have started to call them) have been introduced to the market. The Americans call this material 'graphite', which is really the correct name as there is a difference between carbon and graphite that is used in the manufacture of blanks for fishing rods. These rods are running to a slightly similar pattern as glass rods did when they were first introduced. Some are really very bad and should not be on sale, but others are good and no doubt in the very near future, when all the problems of their manufacture have been solved, we shall have really good carbon fibre rods. Whether they will eventually replace glass is doubtful as the price differential is far too great, but one thing is sure – they will not replace built cane for the discerning fly fisherman so long as Tonkin bamboo is available. Since graphite is still very new, particularly to the United Kingdom market, we will not include it as an influence in the pleasure or success of the angler at this time.

The third most influential new material is monofilament. Before the 1939 War, fly fishermen were using silk worm gut for their leaders, or casts as they were then called. Before gut, he had to use horse hair and this was tied directly on to the shank of the hook when the fly was tied. Salmon flies had gut eyes tied on to the shank of the hook for quite some years at the beginning of the century.

Gradually, during recent years as the silk worm gut industry came to an end in Spain, fly fishermen whether they liked it or not were forced to use monofilament leaders. These have improved greatly from the first which were placed on the market. Not only have the manufacturers of monofilament greatly improved their material but, of equal importance, the tapers and the balance of the leaders have been improved.

A great mistake was originally made with monofilament leaders by copying the same sizes and tapers as had been used with silk worm gut. Gut and monofilament are different not only in their stiffness but, more important, in their weights. As with the fly line, the function of the leader depends on the distribution of the weight. The latest development in monofilament leaders is the continuous tapered leader, which can even be bought treated to sink quickly – ideal for nymph fishing just below the surface.

Nylon monofilament has helped the sea angler, coarse angler and all types of spinning more perhaps than any new material. The recent members to angling would find life very difficult if they had to use the types of lines available to their elders. The

Teach-In on fly fishing

KNOWING the exact fly to use is very often just a case of one-upmanship. It bears no relation to the numbers of fish caught, because most fish will take a reasonably good imitation if the fly is persistently dropped in the right spot.

Picture A: The method of fishing the dry fly. Keep a watch for a rising fish or one which dimples the water-film as it sucks in the 'dry' fly. Cast upstream above the fish, and use only one fly on the leader.

Picture B: The wet-fly fisherman casts his lure downstream, and he may use up to three flies suitably spaced on the nylon leader.

It is customary for wet flies to sink, but dry flies are kept on the surface by a pre-brushing with floatant aerosol.

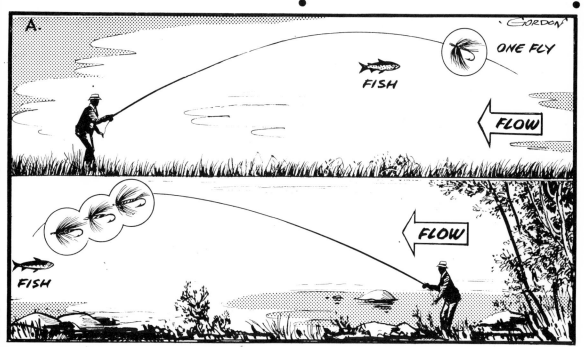

ease of bait and spin casting today has changed out of all recognition from what it was in the days prior to reliable monofilament.

There are many brands of monofilament on the market and the angler himself must find out which is best. Limp soft monofilament does not 'birds nest' as easily as stiffer monofilament when used on a multiplier reel and casts very much smoother and for greater distances; but, being soft, it bruises more easily when knotted, and knots must be pulled up very slowly or·else great heat is generated which can make a weakness in the knot. The best fishing monofilament is always a compromise between stiffness and softness.

The fourth major change of material is that of vinyl coating nylon braided core in the manufacture of fly lines. Today the sale of these lines dominates the market, which was once held exclusively by oil-dressed silk. These vinyl-coated lines can be made to any specific gravity, to float or to sink at varying speeds and depths. Because of the large range of lines on the market, care must be taken that the

Jim Hardy's advice has been sought in all parts of the world, and here are two shots of the former casting champion when he ran a fly fishing school in Japan. He demonstrates casting faults (above) and corrects them (below) before an audience of enthusiastic pupils.

HARDY FLY FISHING SCHOOL

correct weight of line is used on a given rod. The most expensive fly rod in the world will not work correctly unless it carries the weight of line for which it was designed to cast. A fly line must also be supple to behave correctly when cast. Use only smooth supple lines.

All these changes in materials have been developed mainly through a relatively small band of dedicated tournament casters. Many anglers consider tournament casting of no relation to angling, but nothing could be further from the truth. Nearly all the advances made in bait and fly-casting equipment have sprung from the tournament field. Most of the major tackle manufacturers during the past hundred years have developed and proven their new ideas and materials at tournaments. They have all had top-class tournament casters as part of their staff, or retained by them, just as car manufacturers retain top-class drivers. In fact, tournament casting has helped anglers in the same way as motor racing has helped the motorist.

Tournaments are held in many countries, the top casters of each country competing against each other at World tournaments which are held in different countries each year. There are both professional and amateur casters, the professionals usually being retained or employed by a manufacturer. The position of a champion caster is reached only after years of practice and experimenting with tackle.

Every major fishing tackle manufacturer has its own research and development department. Many companies also enlist the help and advice of experienced and specialist anglers, who have spent years improving their skills and techniques. All types of tackle have improved a great deal during the years.

All spinning reels, whether fixed or revolving spool, or closed face, seem always to be improving and changing in design. These are mostly made in Sweden, Germany, France, Japan, United States, Italy and England. Hooks of all types are now nearly all machine made. Hand-made hooks, which do have certain advantages, are now made only in England. Fly lines come mainly from the United States, Germany and England. The most popular brands of monofilament are from the United States, France and Germany. Rods are manufactured in most countries where fishing takes place, but their quality varies a great deal and great care must be taken in their selection. The best-quality fly reels are manufactured in England and exported all over the world.

TEACH-IN on DAPPING

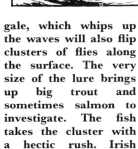

DAPPING is a method of fishing which allows the fly to flit across the water. A good dap hand is kept busy hauling in the big fish, so take no notice of those who say that dapping is the lazy man's way to fish.

Anything, from a gentle wind to a mini gale, which whips up the waves will also flip clusters of flies along the surface. The very size of the lure brings up big trout and sometimes salmon to investigate. The fish takes the cluster with a hectic rush. Irish and Scottish lakes are superb dapping grounds.

Use a 15ft light rod with wide rings. Hold the rod high (see illustration). Silk lines which are made to blow in the wind are not cheap. Make do with embroidery cotton silk floss and tie about 15 yards of it to an ordinary trout reel and line.

Dapping flies are easily made up (A). Large artificial may flies may be tied in tandem (B). Daddy long-legs and gnats gathered from the waterside and hedges can also be clip-hooked. But make the bait big.

Fishing and fishing techniques vary greatly throughout the world, but fly fishing remains, in its various forms, nearly standard. The standards of casting the fly vary enormously throughout the world and although these anglers may be using the finest equipment, in many cases their performance is far below their potential. Happily, as the marketing of fishing tackle improves, casting clinics and angling courses are being used as part of the marketing mix. This helps to bring the brotherhood of anglers together, which is one of the many excellent by-products of angling.

There is room for an enormous amount of teaching of fly casting in many countries and this requires a great deal of skill as the language barrier can be very formidable. It is estimated that there are approximately three million anglers in the United Kingdom and this is growing. In the United States there is somewhere between fifty-five and sixty million, and lately increased interest in angling is taking place in the Middle East Arab countries.

The brotherhood of anglers is really world-wide, and one wonders how much further fishing tackle can yet be improved and what new materials lie ahead for the anglers of the future.

TEACH-IN on ROACH and RUDD

★ ★ ★

ROACH are the most common fish in the British Isles. There are so many in Scottish rivers that the local anglers regard them as vermin.

Experienced anglers sometimes confuse roach with rudd. Picture A shows the difference.

Usually the rudd takes its food near the surface, but a roach will look for its food near the bottom.

A spool of lead fuse wire is often better to use as a weight than tiny lead shot. The wire can be cut into neat lengths as in Picture B.

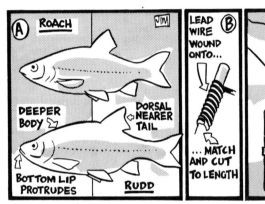

Big roach go for chrysalis bait. When the maggots stop wriggling they gradually turn yellow, orange, red and finally crimson. Anglers call them

'casters'. Black casters are inferior and should be discarded.

Picture C shows you how to make a caster-sieve.

How to mix it!

WARM summer days mean plenty of fresh mackerel and the occasional shark catch for sea anglers.

As bait, Rubby-Dubby (Picture A) is made from dead herrings, fresh mackerel, crabs and offal from the butchers' slaughterhouse.

Pounded together in a bucket and slung in a muslin bag from the stern of the boat (Picture B), it creates a 'smell

trail' which will attract sharks from miles around. Big congers cannot resist a tempting bait made from the head and the trailing entrails of a dead fish (Picture C).

And to keep lugworm, ragworm and apothogel artificial worms whole and natural-looking, just use a hook which has a serrated shank (Picture D).

The fascinating world of

TROPICAL FISH

by CHARLES WADE

STARTING to keep a well-stocked tropical fish tank in the home often springs from the thrilling childhood experience of watching a few minnows in a jar, or the single goldfish in a small bowl. Fish lived for a few short mystified weeks. Every movement in the jar, each trip around the bowl was fascinating to watch. Imagine, then, how much more captivating it can be if a colony of fishes is established.

At the outset, all you will need to buy is a heater, controlled by a thermostat set at 78 degrees, and a tank. Plus, of course, the fish.

Various types of heat-strips are on the market. Basically they consist of a 100-watt element in a heat-resistant glass casing. At the top of the casing, two insulated wires go through a very tight-fitting rubber cork. It is quite safe.

Water should be kept at a regular temperature. Just like human beings, fish dislike a rapid cold spell. Anything below 60 degrees can prove fatal to a tropical fish family. If a power cut does occur, silver foil can be wrapped around the tank to keep the heat in. When it is intended to start the fish breeding, a temperature of 78 to 80 degrees is just about right.

It is folly to start keeping fish with a smallish tank. Therefore buy the biggest you can afford. Surface area is vitally important because the fish take in dissolved oxygen from the water as it passes through behind the gill covers. Without oxygen all fishes suffocate. Depth can be about the same as width.

Rainwater is easily collected. And it is much bet-

ter than tap-water. But if tap-water has to be used, 'soft' water is better than hard. In extreme cases, a powder can be bought from the chemist (or a fish breeder) which sprinkles pepper-pot fashion to increase the acidity or the alkalinity of the water as necessary.

Place the tank out of the strong sun, but in a position where it gets plenty of daylight. It will be heavy enough to require a metal stand or a good strong table.

Well washed sand or fine gravel, and a few small 'rocks' make the aquarium look like a real pool raised to eye level and self-contained. Root plants can be anchored by a stone. Some greenery that floats is also desirable. Apart from providing food for the fishes, the plants will help to prevent algae and scum from forming on the glass. Rooted plants also thrive on fish droppings in the sand.

The choice of plants is a wide one and no harm is done by experimenting with grasses and weed from rivers, ponds and brooks. Some easy-to-buy water plants are cabomba, ceratopteris and cryptocorynes.

A most striking feature of tropical fish is that some of them do not lay eggs. Young broods of fish in batches of 20 to 200 leave the parent as complete fish which measure less than a quarter of an inch. Falling to the bottom of the tank or lodging in the leaves, it is not long before they dart around and seek sanctuary from bigger fish which are often after an easy meal.

To save fish losses, the enthusiastic breeder will have several separate small tanks to which myriads

141

of tiny fish can be transferred by stages. These live-bearing fish are quite hardy, and being generally bigger than egg-bearers, they are most suitable as beginners' stock.

Guppies are prime favourites. Extremely colourful, of every shade, tint and mixture, no two of the male species are alike. The females are a plain sandy grey. Average length is 1–1¼in. In-breeding by experts has given us a range of guppies as diverse as types of roses. Gold guppy and lace guppy are community-loving fish which peacefully share territory. We also have scarf tails, sword tails, and double sword tails.

Mollies grow to a length of 2½–3in, with black the most popular colour. A rather uncommon fish which poses no problems for beginners is the **Merry Widow**. Not fussy about food, it is never still and it makes quick darts hither and thither. **Platys** are also a good fish to try. They love to feed on the green algae which forms on plants and at the sides of the glass. But they are also cannibalistic.

Egg-bearing species of tropical fish far outnumber the 'live-young' bearers and each type of fish lays a different type of egg. Some will hatch out in less than a day, and others will take as long as six months. Pairs of spawning fish take up a position side-by-side, and trembling together at the vents, the female releases a batch of eggs and the male immediately exudes a fine cloud of milt which envelopes the eggs in a fertilising process.

A magnifying glass gives a good view of some eggs which stick to plants. Each stage of growth and hatch-out can be observed just as frog-spawn is seen to develop – but of course it is not so involved a process.

With thousands of egg-bearing fish to choose from, it would be fatal to introduce any that turn out to be bullying to others or incompatible in the

IT'S A BITING WINTER!

The leaves have gone from the trees but fishing a lake in winter can still be productive. This angler fished for bream with two maggots to a size 16 hook. Note how he carefully plays the fish on leger tackle and that his keepnet is ready and close by his feet to hold the catch. The lake is at Mote Park in Maidstone – a low-priced day ticket water.

aquarium. A small selection of suitable fish for all enthusiasts could be glass fish, zebra, neon tetra, bronze catfish, harlequin and angel fish.

Glass fish are transparent and prefer live food. **Zebras** are a beautiful silver colour, with horizontal deep-blue stripes all along the body. **Neon tetra** are the best from a group of tetras. The forepart of the belly is of purest white, a blue-green line streaks along the body, and the rear is tinged with red.

Catfish are scavengers – but beautiful, and necessary to every tank. One fish is sufficient to keep the tank pure. Digging down into the sand, it will devour greedily each particle of food not eaten by other occupants. The catfish lives most of its life along the gravel bottom, and a rare and fascinating quick dash to the surface for a mouthful of oxygen is a sight not to be missed.

Harlequins prefer to live and move in shoals. Shaded with gold, they carry a dark-blue triangle on the flanks.

Angel fish come in three types, silver with black bars, black laced and pure black. They show a tendency for sulking and it is not uncommon for odd ones to lie down and die. The body is round and extremely flat; its shape is commonly chosen for drawings and artwork which is intended to convey the popular image of tropical fish shapes.

To feed the fish, small worms or particles of dried food should be spread very thinly all over the tank so that all fish get a fair share. Most fish are gluttons and they should be underfed rather than overfed.

A change of diet will appeal to the fish. Water insects scooped from the surface of a pond or from the top of a rainwater barrel are easily collected, and greatly relished by the fish. But watch out for leeches and the larvae of dragon fly which might be introduced accidentally with harmless natural foods. Snails have their uses in a colony of fish, but as they multiply so rapidly it is questionable whether they should be introduced at all.

Fish do fall ill from time to time. If the water becomes chilled, resistance of the fish is lowered, and it is then that parasites burrow under the scales and into the gills. White spot is the most decimating disease of all and it relatively common and contagious. All new fish should be quarantined for a period. Aquatic plants should be washed clean before introduction to the water.

Methylene blue is often used to 'immerse' fish which are blotched with disease in commercial trout hatcheries. Used sparingly, and diluted to a very pale blue, it may cure and also prevent white spot.

Fungus, dropsy, neon and other wasting diseases are not disastrous. A better supply of oxygen soon restores the stock to a healthy state.

Other minor additions to the decor of a tank are strip lighting over the top, which should be switched off during the normal hours of darkness, and a net or grid discreetly placed to prevent energetic specimens from leaping only to die on the carpet.

To watch fish swimming is excellent therapy. In this modern age we all need to stand back and stare. Nature is never more soothing than when observed in the wonderful world of the aquarium.

DON'T LET THE OARS SAIL AWAY!

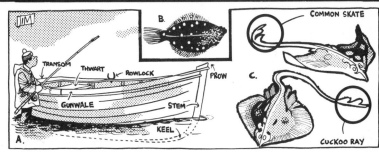

FEEL SAFE in a sturdy boat. It may be a clinker, as in Picture A, or the more modern fibreglass type.

Make sure the oars fit properly into the row-locks. And, of course, secure the oars and row-locks with a loose cord to the thwarts for safety.

Always carry emergency flares and a whistle. Boat rods are quite short because no casting-out is needed.

Plaice (Picture B) are highly-prized fish. Return all small ones to the water – they will add three inches in a single year.

Skate and ray (Picture C) are **diamond-shaped fish which feed near the bottom of the sea and smother the prey. Keep clear of the tails. They whiplash when the fish are flopping in the boat.**

And if you like to end with a good tail, how about this one?

A fine conger eel taken from Scottish waters off Stornoway. It fell to a whole mackerel bait that was caught on feathers. The angler holding the eel won a Southern Television 'Out of Town' championship. Who could wish for a longer conger?